Swimming – A Train

David Wright & Jane Copland

Swimming
A Training Program

Meyer & Meyer Sport

British Library Cataloguing in Publication Data
A catalogue record for this book is available from the British Library

Wright, David & Copland, Jane:
Swimming – A Training Program
Oxford: Meyer & Meyer Sport (UK) Ltd., 2004
ISBN 1-84126-142-4

Aachen, Adelaide, Auckland, Budapest, Graz, Johannesburg,
Miami, Olten (CH), Oxford, Singapore, Toronto
Member of the World
Sports Publishers' Association (WSPA)
www.w-s-p-a.org
Printed and bound by: FINIDR, s. r. o., Český Těšín
ISBN 1-84126-142-4
E-Mail: verlag@m-m-sports.com
www.m-m-sports.com

CONTENTS

PRELUDE

Our first book, "Swim to the Top" included a prelude that described the background and experience of Coach David Wright. In "Swimming – A Training Program" he expands on this with a short story on swimming from the days of his youth.

TO SWIM IN THE POOL OF A GOD

Not many people have been to Te Reinga. It's on the inland road between Wairoa and Gisborne. The main road runs along the coast and has lots of fast cars. The inland road wriggles up valleys with names like Ruakaturi and along a river called Hangaroa and around a mountain called Whakapunaki. And where the Ruakaturi and the Hangaroa meet and right below Whakapunaki, that's Te Reinga.

It is maybe a dozen homes, an abandoned trucking business, a three-room school and a marae. But most important it has the Te Reinga Falls and it is the home of Hinekorako, the only female God of the Maori.

In 1350 the last of the great waka from eastern Polynesia, Takitimu made landfall on the coast, east of Te Reinga, at Mahia. The purpose of the expedition was to introduce the sacred lore of Hawaiki to Aotearoa. Atua or deities had been captured in wood and stone and were brought to Aotearoa in the waka. One of the atua was Hinekorako. Initially she lived with her people on the marae at Te Reinga. She married and agreed to become a mother on the condition that her husband would always tend to the baby. This was not work for a god. One day during an important meeting of marae elders, he refused and Hinekorako left him and dived into the falls and lives in the cave beneath them to this day.

This might seem like the dull and dusty remnants of myth and fable, but to me it was once very important. You see I was raised in Te Reinga and I was obsessed with swimming. These were the days when O'Brien and Berry from Australia and Scholander from the United States were winning the Olympic Games and Chapman, Shripston and Whittelston represented New Zealand. Cook Strait was still waiting to be swum and Hawke's Bay boasted New Zealand's best swimmers, Palmer, Christie, Meade, Todd and Coutts. I trained in the river just above the Te Reinga falls and raced my mates across its thirty meters. Winning depended on how quickly you could get your feet out of the mud at the start. If only they had needed that skill at Mexico City.

Just as important, many years earlier as Hinekorako left the marae for the last time, she said no male would be a warrior unless he could swim the full length of the narrow channel below the Te Reinga Falls and climb the rock to her cave home. This was difficult, the wide river above the falls narrowed to a rapid ten-meter wide, one hundred and fifty meter long torrent below the falls. Swimming against the current was only the first problem. It was then necessary to swim under the huge volume of falling water and climb the rock. The return journey didn't appear too tough, slide down the rock and rest as the current carried you along the narrow channel and out into the big lake at the end.

As the years went by I swam for Hawke's Bay and won the Auckland and Wellington Winter Swimming Championships. I was second to the New Zealand Champion twice across Lake Taupo, and had won the popular Lake Wiritoa swim. But I had never swum the Te Reinga Falls. Worse, I had looked at it several times and had determined before getting near the water that the swim was impossible. Twice I got into the water but gave up as I felt the pressure of the current and saw the blackness of its depth.

And then in the summer of 1968 I flew to Australia and trained with Don Talbot. I swam with and talked to his Olympic Champions and world record holders. The distances we swam were modest by today's standards but for me they were immense. Back in Te Reinga I looked again at the Te Reinga Falls. Surely now I could meet Hinekorako's challenge. I was lucky, 1968 had been a dry summer and the volume of water was lower than normal – perhaps, tomorrow.

Donald came with me and we climbed down the bush path to the end of the channel. We sat for a while on the rock ledge and discussed strategy. Goggles were a new thing in those days and I would wear them. I would swim on the left because a rock at the top of the channel made the current weaker on that side. I got into the water and wondered why swiftly flowing water always seemed colder than gentle currents. Like wind, does water have a chill factor?

The first portion of the swim was remarkably easy. I could see the stone bank passing by quite quickly and the effort was not great. Donald had told me to watch for the rock that broke the current but I forgot and swam into it. The current on the other side was much faster. Now it was hard work. But you know how in a race there sometimes is a moment when the brain says," I'm going to do this." Well that's what it was like at Te Reinga. I reached the edge of the falling water and swam in underneath. The weight of water was similar to a breaking wave and pushed me under. It did not take long though and I was on the other side, behind the veil of a God. The climb to the cave was easy and soon I sat on the doorstep of Hinekorako's home.

Now, do you want to know two really silly things?

Hinekorako said, you became a warrior completing that swim and just for a couple of minutes, sitting behind the waterfall, she was right. And second, ever so occasionally when I see Thorpe or Klim or Huegill or Hackett breaking a world record or winning a world title, I hear a little voice asking, "Ah, but could they swim the Te Reinga Falls?"

R
G
SPEEDO

INTRODUCTION

HOW TO USE THE BOOK AND ITS SCHEDULES

Our first book "Swim to the Top" describes how Lydiard's system of training can be applied successfully to competitive swimming. It is a general book that addresses the principles of the swimming program. It does not however detail the schedules involved in putting Lydiard's principles into practice. This second book, "Swimming – A Training Program" takes the next step. It sets out the 300 swimming schedules and 115 weight schedules making up a single six-month training cycle.

To be most effective "Swimming – A Training Program" should be read in association with "Swim to the Top". One provides the training practice and the other the training theory. However, for readers who have not been able to access a copy of "Swim to the Top" each chapter in "Swimming – A Training Program" begins with a summary of the theory supporting the schedules that follow. Each week's program, which in most cases involves thirteen swimming schedules and five weight schedules, also includes a description of how the week's program is compatible with and contributes to Lydiard's training objectives.

There is no reason why experienced swimmers cannot follow the schedules exactly as they are included in the book. A better way, however, is to look at what each schedule is trying to achieve and how it does it, and then swim either the schedule suggested or some modified version that better suits the swimmer. Before making a change, make sure the principle behind the schedule is not being compromised. Turning a long aerobic conditioning workout into a series of 25m sprints or a kick session into a medley workout will upset the balance of the recommended program and the swimmer's final result.

Don't use the schedules like one coach who rang me and said he wanted a "Lydiard training session." I asked him why he wanted just one session. Training programs do not work that way. Each session needs to relate to every other session so that the season forms an integrated whole. Wednesday's training needs to take into account the training done on Tuesday and planned for Thursday. Week Five's training needs to take into account the training done in

Week Four and planned for Week Six. Each individual session needs to reflect and assist in achieving the season's main competitive goal. He told me that all the different training ideas were confusing him, so he had decided he would get a Lydiard type schedule from me for Monday's training, an interval session from a specialist interval coach for Tuesday and so on through the week. His squad would be getting a balanced portion of everybody's ideas – it just had to work. I couldn't believe it so I just gave him Week Five's Saturday morning Waitakeres session. All that was a couple of years ago now and I haven't heard of a host of champions coming from his squad, so I guess his idea of a balanced program needs to be reviewed.

The next few chapters address the training schedules involved in each of the race preparation stages of a Lydiard program. For example the next chapter covers the Aerobic Build-up period: the following chapter, the Transition period, then the Anaerobic Conditioning period and finally, the Trials and Coordination period. The table below shows the number of swimming and weight training schedules included in "Swimming – A Training Program" for each of these periods.

PERIOD	WEEKS	SWIM SCHEDULES	WEIGHT SCHEDULES
Build-up	10	130	50
Transition	1	13	5
Anaerobic	4	52	20
Trials & C	10	105	40
Totals	25	300	115

Younger And Less Experienced Swimmers

Less experienced swimmers, not yet able to handle the full Lydiard program, will need to modify the schedules to bring them down to a volume that they can manage. How this is best done will depend on whether swimmers are less experienced because they are young athletes just setting out on their senior competitive careers or recreational swimmers who use swimming as part of their fitness program or triathletes who have to allocate training time to three disciplines or surf swimmers using pool work to prepare for their specialist sport. The demands and requirements of each category are very different. To assist in adapting the competitive pool schedules in this book, I have included suggestions at the end of each week's training notes on how they can be modified for younger swimmers, recreational swimmers and triathletes. For example, should the number of repetitions or the length of each repetition be reduced. The answer is you can usually do either, but the notes will give you guidance.

CHAPTER ONE
THE BUILD-UP SCHEDULES

The function of a build-up is widely misunderstood. It is a period of training that is not distance, stroke or race specific. It is equally relevant to 50m or 1500m freestyle or 200m butterfly. An analogy might help clarify its purpose.

Companies involved in the forestry industry can operate in one of two ways. They can cut down trees to be used in their mills without replanting the forests behind them. While they are cutting, the mills work well and profits are high. Eventually the trees are all cut, the resources have been used and the mills close. A prudent company however plants one and a half hectares of new trees for every hectare cut. When the first company is closing the other has more resources than when it started. Short-term profits have been reduced by the cost of replanting, but without it there is no long-term business. Swimming is the same. The build-up is the swimmer's time of replanting. It is the period in which athletes increase their resources – resources that are equally beneficial whether the swimmer competes over 50m, 200m or 1500m.

Like the forestry company analogy the value of a build-up is not immediately apparent. Real deep-seated benefits take time to evolve. Over five or six seasons however they produce results their "clear-felled" peers will not be able to match. Be very aware, however, that results in the early seasons may take longer to show than aggressively sprint trained competitors. Build-up conditioning is not the fastest way of achieving fine results. In fact it is often quite slow. It is, however, the best way to achieve the best results.

The table below summarizes the daily distances making up each week's build-up schedule. The weekly mileage has been set at 100 kilometers. Experience has shown this produces similar physiological demands on a swimmer as 100 miles per week does on a runner. It is a distance that is taxing, but can still be managed at speeds close to the top aerobic range. If the distance swum each week is much below 100km it can be swum at good aerobic speeds but is not taxing enough to achieve the finest aerobic development. If the distance is too long, the swimmer's speed reduces to a plod and again aerobic conditioning suffers. The ideal distance is the maximum that can be swum at the athlete's best possible aerobic pace. All individuals are different and therefore the best distance will vary from swimmer to swimmer. In general, however, 100km each week appears to be a good best average. However, I can well imagine some top athletes, especially women swimmers completing 120+km per week at the required effort. The table also shows the timing of Week Five's weight training sessions. The weight training days can be varied if some other timetable suits the swimmer better.

BUILD-UP – WEEKLY PROGRAM

DAY	AM/PM	PER SESSION DISTANCE-KM	PER DAY DISTANCE-KM	WEIGHT SESSIONS
MONDAY	AM	6.0mr		
	PM	8.0mr	14.0	——
TUESDAY	AM	7.5k		
	PM	10.0l	17.5	Weights
WED.	AM	8.0m		
	PM	6.0hl	14.0	Weights
THUR.	AM	7.5k		
	PM	10.0l	17.5	Weights
FRIDAY	AM	6.0mr		
	PM	8.0mr	14.0	Weights
SATURDAY	AM	10.0w		
	PM	5.0sc	15.0	——
SUNDAY	AM	8.0mr		
	PM	——	8.0	Weights
TOTALS		100	100	5

Codes

mr Sessions whose main purpose is to aid recovery from the week's harder swims. None of this swimming should be hard and is broken up to include a mixture of kicking, swimming, pull and drills.

k Sessions where the emphasis is on kick sets. In a 7.5km session up to 4km is done as kick with fins.

l These are key sessions of long, firm aerobic swimming. In a 10km session 2km should be warm-up, 2km should be warm-down and 6km should be firm aerobic swimming of repetitions between 500m and 3000m.

m Sessions where the main emphasis is on medley swimming. Medleys can range in length from 100m up to a build-up favorite 4000m.

hl "Hill" sessions of 25m repeats with 25m easy between for technique development. Swimmers must not sprint this session. Good technique is the session's purpose.

w "Waitakeres" usually 100x100m or similar. The session has the same aerobic conditioning purpose as the long sessions.

Note

The recomended weight program involves twenty-four seperate exercises divided into four groups of six exercises. The swimmer starts with Session One and works through to Session Four before returning to Session One again. This allows four or five days rest between repititions of the same group of exercises – an important factor in improving strength and avoiding weight training injuries.

WEEK ONE SCHEDULES

Week One – Monday AM – 6000 Mixed			
Warm-up	1000	Kick, With Fins Your Choice	
Swim	5 x 200	Done As	1) Butterfly 2) Backstroke 3) Breaststroke 4) Freestyle 5) Individual Medley
Kick	1000	Kick, With Fins Your Choice	
Swim	10 x 100	Freestyle – 15 sec. Interval	
Kick	1000	Done As	200 Breaststroke Kick 800 No Fins Your Choice
Swim	20 x 50	Done As	5 x 50 Each Stroke

Week One – Monday PM – 8000 Individual Medley

Set One – No Fins
1000 Freestyle Pull
700 Backstroke Swim
200 Breaststroke Swim
100 Breaststroke Kick

Set Two – With Fins
1000 Butterfly / Butterfly Drills
700 Freestyle Kick
200 Backstroke Kick
100 Butterfly Kick

Set Three – No Fins
1000 Freestyle Pull
700 Backstroke Pull
200 Breaststroke Swim
100 Breaststroke Kick

Set Four – With Fins
1000 Individual Medley
700 Freestyle Kick
200 Backstroke Kick
100 Butterfly Kick

Week One – Tuesday AM – 7500 Kick		
Warm-up	1500	Swim, No Fins Your Choice
	1000	Kick, With Fins Your Choice
Swim	5x100	Butterfly
Kick	200	Butterfly, No Fins
	300	Butterfly, With Fins
Swim	5x100	Backstroke
Kick	200	Backstroke, No Fins
	300	Backstroke, With Fins
Swim	5x100	Breaststroke
Kick	500	Breaststroke
Swim	5x100	Freestyle
Kick	200	Freestyle, No Fins
	300	Freestyle, With Fins
Warm-down	1000	Swim, With Fins Your Choice

Week One – Tuesday PM – 10,000 Long		
Warm-up	1000	Kick, With Fins Your Choice
	1000	Swim, No Fins Your Choice
Main Set	3x500	Freestyle Swim
	3x500	Freestyle Pull
	2x500	Breaststroke Swim
	2x500	Backstroke Swim
	2x500	Backstroke Pull
Warm-down	1000	Kick, With Fins Your Choice
	1000	Swim, With Fins Your Choice

Week One – Tuesday – Weights

Session One

- Pull Down Behind
- Chin Ups
- Flies
- Wrist Curls
- Forearm Pull Downs
- Sit Ups
- 15min. Bike

Week One – Wednesday AM – 8000 Mixed

Warm-up	1000	Kick, With Fins Your Choice
	1000	Swim, No Fins Your Choice
	1000	Pull, No Fins Your Choice
Main Set	32x100	Individual Medley – 15 sec Interval
Warm-down	1000	Kick, With Fins Your Choice
	800	Swim, With Fins Your Choice

Week One – Wednesday PM – 6000 Mixed

Warm-up	500	Kick, With Fins Your Choice
	500	Swim, No Fins Your Choice
	500	Pull, No Fins Your Choice
Main Set	1500	Butterfly/Butterfly Drills Your Choice
	1500	Backstroke, Pull
Warm-down	1000	Kick, With Fins Your Choice
	500	Swim, With Fins Your Choice

Week One – Wednesday – Weights

Session Two

- Pull Down Front
- Curls
- Elbow Raises
- Two Form Dips
- Back Lifts
- Squats
- 15min. Bike

Week One – Thursday AM – 7500 Kick		
Warm-up	1500	Swim, No Fins Your Choice
	1500	Pull, No Fins Your Choice
Main Set	3000	Kick, With Fins Your Choice
	500	Kick, No Fins, Min.100 Breaststroke
Warm-down	1000	Swim, With Fins Your Choice

Week One – Thursday PM – 10,000 Long		
Warm-up	1000	Kick, With Fins Your Choice
	1000	Swim, No Fins Your Choice
Main Set	2x1500	Swim, Freestyle
	1x1500	Pull, Freestyle
	1x1500	Swim, Backstroke
Warm-down	1000	Kick, With Fins Your Choice
	1000	Swim, With Fins Your Choice

Week One – Thursday – Weights

Session Three

- Pull Down Front
- Dips
- Dumb Bell Behind Head
- Machine Pull Together
- Tricep Push Downs
- Leg Raises
- 15min. Bike

Week One – Friday AM – 6000 Mixed			
Swim	1000		
Kick	1500	With Fins Your Choice	
Pull	1000		
Swim	1000	Individual Medley	
		Done As	100 Butterfly
			200 Individual Medley
			100 Backstroke
			200 Individual Medley
			100 Breaststroke
			200 Individual Medley
			100 Freestyle
Kick	1500	With Fins Your Choice	

Week One – Friday PM – 8000 Medley		
Set One	2000	Swim, Freestyle, No Fins
	1200	Kick, Freestyle, With Fins
	800	Pull, Freestyle, No Fins
Set Two	1400	Swim, Backstroke, No Fins
	800	Kick, Backstroke, With Fins
	400	Pull, Backstroke, No Fins
Set Three	800	Swim, Individual Medley, No Fins
	400	Kick, Individual Medley, With Fins Except Breaststroke
	200	Swim, Individual Medley, No Fins

Week One – Friday – Weights

Session Four

- Seated Rows
- Bench Press
- Bend Over Rows
- Machine Push Aparts
- Cleans
- Hamstrings
- 15min. Bike

Week One – Saturday AM – 10,000 Waitakeres		
Kick	2000	With Fins Your Choice
Swim	30x100	Freestyle – 15 sec Recovery
Kick	2000	With Fins Your Choice
Pull	30x100	Freestyle – 15 sec Recovery

Week One – Saturday PM – 5000 Kick			
Warm-up	1000 1000	Kick, With Fins Your Choice Swim, No Fins Your Choice	
Drills	500		
Stroke Correction	800		
Kick	3x400	With Fins,	1) Freestyle 2) Backstroke 3) Butterfly
Kick	500	Breaststroke	

Week One – Sunday AM – 8000 Mixed		
Warm-up	2000	No Fins Your Choice
Swim	20x50	Freestyle, No Fins
Kick	2000	With Fins Your Choice
Swim	20x50	Breaststroke
Pull	2000	No Fins Your Choice

Week One – Sunday – Weights

Session One

- Pull Down Behind
- Chin Ups
- Flies
- Wrist Curls
- Forearm Pull Downs
- Sit Ups
- 15min. Bike

NOTES TO WEEK ONE SCHEDULES

Several schedules in the build-up, such as those on Monday, Friday and Sunday are recovery sessions where the good is in the mileage swum, mileage for mileage's sake. That's not a politically correct thing to say about a training program. Today everything has to have more meaning than that. Well in this case, there is nothing wrong with clocking up kilometers just for the aerobic benefit kilometers provide. Swimmers used to a seven days per week distance conditioning program find these days aid recovery more than a day off. After a day off, swimmers start the following day stiff and sore. Their muscles are still feeling the effects of the long taxing swims. It takes them a further day of swimming just to loosen up again.

Too Much catch-up

Nicole demonstrates a typical catch-up stroke – where the recovery arm catches up with the pulling arm. I prefer the 180 degree alternating stroke.

180 apart

Nicole demonstrates the 180 degree alternating stroke. This is the freestyle I prefer.

The key 10km "long" sessions are swum on Tuesday, Thursday and Saturday. They are the swimming equivalent of Lydiard's long two-hour runs. The main sets should be timed and the times recorded to be compared with the same main sets when they are swum again in the second five weeks of the build-up. Remember, although the sets are timed, they must be swum aerobically. Going anaerobic may produce impressive training times but contributes little to the aerobic objectives of the build-up.

Saturday morning's training is the week's third 10km "long" session and in recognition of its Lydiard origins is called the Waitakeres. This was the range of hills in the west of Auckland where each week Lydiard tested his runners over a rugged 22-mile circuit. Every Saturday's "Waitakeres" session is based around 100m repetitions that culminate in Weeks Five and Nine with 100x100m with a 15 seconds interval. The length of the rest is based on research done on runners in Finland that established a rest of 15 seconds or less did not affect the aerobic nature of the session. It avoids the 100x100m becoming a session of hard anaerobic repetitions. 100x100m done this way is physiologically the same as a 10km straight swim.

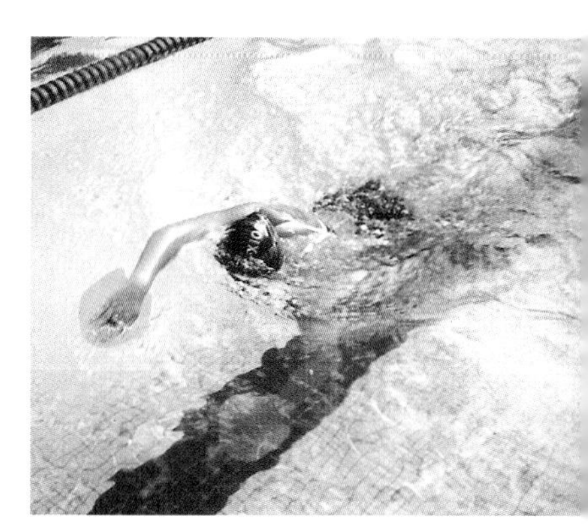

Hand Paddles

Nicole demonstrates the use of hand paddles – a useful tool for improving swimmers arm strength and correcting some faults such as slipping.

Kicking

Nicole finishes another length kick. Spend time on conditioning a swimmer's kick. If a swimmer's kick fails, the rest of the stroke will soon follow.

Saturday afternoon's session is important because it sets aside time specifically for stroke correction. Stroke correction should be part of every training session. When faults are detected they should be corrected irrespective of whether stroke correction is mentioned in the schedule. Nevertheless it is good to set aside one session each week when time is specifically allocated to stroke correction. It means once a week both coach and swimmers are obliged to specifically address the question of technique. It should ensure faults do not carry on by default.

Don't correct stroke characteristics just because they look odd. Evaluate whether what looks like a fault actually matters. Frequently some quite odd-looking things don't affect the swimmer's efficiency – if the swimmer feels comfortable swimming that way, leave it alone. One of my best sprinters, Nichola Chellingworth, had a strange kink in her wrist when she recovered her left arm swimming freestyle, but her hand entered the water normally. The only reason for changing it would have been to avoid having to constantly respond to well meaning onlookers asking, "Why does Nichola have that strange kink in her wrist?" Evaluate what is a stroke fault and what is just a stroke idiosyncrasy and correct the faults.

Sunday's single swimming session includes two sets of 20x50m, which at first may appear quite contrary to Lydiard's principles of build-up conditioning. However, they are included as an extension of Saturday's stroke correction tuition. Swimming these 50m slowly provides an opportunity to drill Saturday's technique lesson.

This week sees the first weight training sessions of the new season. Be cautious about the amount of weight lifted. The purpose of weight training at this stage is just to get the body back into weight training condition. There is plenty of time to load up the weights. Doing so too early could cause injury and will almost certainly leave the swimmer unnecessarily stiff and sore. To start with, lift weights the swimmer feels are too light. Even then swimmers may be a little stiff from the early sessions. The happy thought is that this will probably get worse for two or three days before muscles adjust to the new season's training. A little stiffness should not be used as a reason for missing training.

Annie and Fara

Annie and Fara complete an eight kilometer sea swim. These events are terrific conditioning for pool swimmers

Each weight exercise should be done as three sets of seven repetitions with the exception of sit-ups, which should be done as a single set of 500. I arrived at seven repetitions after experimenting for several years with repetitions of between three and twenty. The number that contributes most to the swimmer's strength is seven. Fewer repetitions than this generate good strength gains, but produce too much muscle bulk. More than seven repetitions and the weight lifted needs to be reduced with corresponding lower strength gains.

Sunday's weight training session is the beginning of the second cycle of weights. Swimmers can now increase the weights lifted by increasing each exercise by one weight increment. For example, in our local gym the dumb bells increase in weight in two-kilogram increments. If a swimmer has done flies with 24 kilograms in cycle one, I would increase this to 26 kilograms in cycle two. For those exercises involving machine weights, our gym's machines increase their weights in seven-kilogram increments. A swimmer lifting 42 kilograms in cycle one should aim to lift 49 kilograms in cycle two.

YOUNGER AND LESS EXPERIENCED SWIMMERS

A full Lydiard program is not intended for junior pre-teen swimmers setting out on their swimming career. At this stage swimming should be only one of a range of activities. Swimming the schedules in this book allows time for sleep and school or part-time work but can not accommodate anything like the diversity that should be part of a young pre-teen's life. Children should be allowed the time to be children. Their lives should be full of diverse and interesting activity. If, however, a swimming career based on a Lydiard training program becomes an athlete's thing, it will be done better looking back on an early childhood that involved lots of other interests. It's a choice between an athlete who thinks," The only thing I've ever done is swim." or, "I tried heaps of things but the one I liked best was swimming." It's fairly certain which will give the best result.

WEEK TWO SCHEDULES

Week Two – Monday AM – 6000 Mixed			
Warm-up	1000	Kick, With Fins Your Choice	
Swim	5 x 200	Done As	1) Butterfly 2) Backstroke 3) Breaststroke 4) Freestyle 5) Individual Medley
Kick	1000	Kick, With Fins Your Choice	
Swim	10 x 100	Backstroke	
Kick	1000	Done As	200 Breaststroke 800 No Fins Your Choice
Swim	20 x 50	Done As	5 x 50 Each Stroke

Week Two – Monday PM – 8000 Individual Medley

Set One – No Fins
2000 Backstroke Swim

Set Two – With Fins
1000 Butterfly / Butterfly Drills
500 Freestyle Kick
300 Backstroke Kick
200 Butterfly Kick

Set Three – No Fins
2000 Freestyle Pull

Set Four – With Fins
1000 Individual Medley
500 Freestyle Kick
300 Backstroke Kick
200 Butterfly Kick

Week Two – Tuesday AM – 7500 Kick		
Warm-up	2000	Swim, No Fins Your Choice
Kick	9x300	With Fins, Done As 1) Freestyle 2) Backstroke, Freestyle, Butterfly x 100 3) Freestyle 4) Backstroke 5) Backstroke, Freestyle, Butterfly x 100 6) Backstroke 7) Butterfly 8) Backstroke, Freestyle, Butterfly x 100 9) Butterfly
Swim, Kick, Drill	8x100	No Fins, Done As 1) Breaststroke 2) Breaststroke 3) Delayed Breaststroke 4) Breaststroke Kick 5) Breaststroke 6) Breaststroke 7) Delayed Breaststroke 8) Breaststroke Kick
Warm-down	1000 1000	Kick, With Fins Your Choice Swim, With Fins Your Choice

Week Two – Tuesday PM – 10,000 Long		
Warm-up	1000 1000	Kick, With Fins Your Choice Swim, No Fins Your Choice
Main Set	5x400 4x400 2x400 2x400 2x400	Freestyle Swim Freestyle Pull Breaststroke Swim Backstroke Swim Backstroke Pull
Warm-down	1000 1000	Kick, With Fins Your Choice Swim, With Fins Your Choice

Week Two – Tuesday – Weights

Session Two

- Pull Down Front
- Curls
- Elbow Raises
- Two Form Dips
- Back Lifts
- Squats
- 15min. Bike

Week Two – Wednesday AM – 8000 Mixed

Warm-up	1500	Kick, With Fins Your Choice
	1500	Swim
Swim	20x50	Butterfly
Main Set	1x400	Individual Medley
	500	Kick, No Fins, Min.100 Breaststroke
	2x200	Breaststroke
	500	Kick, No Fins, Min.100 Breaststroke
	2x100	Breaststroke
Swim	20x50	Backstroke
Warm-down	500	Kick, With Fins Your Choice
	500	Swim, With Fins Your Choice

Week Two – Wednesday PM – 6000 Mixed

Warm-up	500	Kick, With Fins Your Choice
	500	Swim
	500	Pull
Main Set	1500	Breaststroke, With Fins, Butterfly Kick
	1500	Freestyle, Pull
Warm-down	1000	Kick, With Fins Your Choice
	500	Swim, With Fins Your Choice

Week Two – Wednesday – Weights

Session Three

- Pull Down Front
- Dips
- Dumb Bell Behind Head
- Machine Pull Together
- Tricep Push Downs
- Leg Raises
- 15min. Bike

Week Two – Thursday AM – 7500 Kick

Warm-up	1500	Swim, No Fins Your Choice	
	1500	Pull, No Fins Your Choice	
Main Set	4x300	Kick, Each 300 Done As	100 Freestyle 100 Backstroke 100 Butterfly
	6x300	Kick, Done As	1) 300 Freestyle 2) 300 Backstroke 3) 300 Butterfly 4) 300 Freestyle 5) 300 Backstroke 6) 300 Butterfly
	500	Kick, No Fins, Min.100 Breaststroke	
Warm-down	1000	Swim, With Fins Your Choice	

Week Two – Thursday PM – 10,000 Long

Warm-up	1000	Kick, With Fins Your Choice
	1000	Swim, No Fins Your Choice
Main Set	2x1000	Swim, Freestyle
	1x1000	Pull, Freestyle
	1x1000	Swim, Individual Medley
	1x1000	Swim, Backstroke
	1x1000	Pull, Backstroke
Warm-down	1000	Kick, With Fins Your Choice
	1000	Swim, With Fins Your Choice

Week Two – Thursday – Weights

Session Four

- Seated Rows
- Bench Press
- Bend Over Rows
- Machine Push Aparts
- Cleans
- Hamstrings
- 15min. Bike

Week Two – Friday AM – 6000 Mixed

Swim	1000	No Fins Your Choice
Kick	1500	With Fins Your Choice
Pull	1000	No Fins Your Choice
Swim	1000	Individual Medley, With Fins Your Choice Done As 100 Butterfly 200 Individual Medley 100 Backstroke 200 Individual Medley 100 Breaststroke 200 Individual Medley 100 Freestyle
Kick	1500	With Fins Your Choice

Week Two – Friday PM – 8000 Medley

Set One	4x1000	1) Swim, Freestyle 2) Swim, Backstroke 3) Pull, Freestyle 4) Pull, Backstroke
Set Two	4x700	1) Kick, Freestyle, With Fins 2) Kick, Backstroke, With Fins 3) Kick, Butterfly, With Fins 4) Kick, Freestyle, With Fins
Set Three	4x200	Swim, Individual Medley
Set Four	4x100	Swim, Breaststroke

Week Two – Friday – Weights

Session One

- Pull Down Behind
- Chin Ups
- Flies
- Wrist Curls
- Forearm Pull Downs
- Sit Ups
- 15min. Bike

Week Two – Saturday AM – 10,000 Waitakeres

Warm-up	1000	Kick, With Fins Your Choice
	1000	Swim, No Fins Your Choice
Main Set	4x100	Butterfly, With Fins
	8x100	Breaststroke
	16x100	Backstroke, Pull
Kick	1000	Kick, With Fins Your Choice
Main Set	32x100	Freestyle, Pull
Warm-down	1000	Swim, With Fins Your Choice

Week Two – Saturday PM – 5000 Kick

Warm-up	1000	Kick, With Fins Your Choice	
	1000	Swim, No Fins Your Choice	
Drills	500		
Stroke Correction	800		
Kick	3x400	With Fins	1) Freestyle
			2) Backstroke
			3) Butterfly
Kick	500	Breaststroke	

Week Two – Sunday AM – 8000 Mixed		
Warm-up	2000	Your Choice
Swim	20x50	Butterfly
Kick	2000	With Fins Your Choice
Swim	20x50	Backstroke
Pull	2000	Your Choice

Week Two – Sunday – Weights

Session Two

- Pull Down Front
- Curls
- Elbow Raises
- Two Form Dips
- Back Lifts
- Squats
- 15min. Bike

NOTES TO WEEK TWO SCHEDULES

Swimmers are usually feeling quite pleased with themselves at this stage. They have got through the first week and 100kms are safely stored away. The real trick in a Lydiard program, however, is that its effects are cumulative. After the first week, "I'm feeling quite good." After the second week, "I'm feeling pretty tired." By week three,"I don't think I'm going to make this." and in week four," I'm definitely not going to make this." Then in week five or six,"This is beginning to feel a bit better," and by week ten, "No problem, piece of cake. Don't know what all the fuss was about." And you know what; your aerobic base has just got a whole lot better than it was ten weeks ago. So when you're going through the pretty awful stage, hang in there, it will come right. The other thing all this highlights is you have to do the ten weeks. One week is easy. In fact it amuses me the Clubs that go away for a one-week training camp and swim 100kms. Lydiard did not arrive at the figure of ten weeks aerobic conditioning by chance. He arrived at it because that's what it takes.

Tuesday afternoon's training is the fourth "long" session. A variety of repetition distances, making up the six kilometers of the main set, have been selected based on the principle that the swimmers general aerobic condition will be best improved by experiencing a range of aerobic experiences. Generally, the Tuesday sessions contain shorter repeat distances, the Thursday sessions, longer distances and the Saturday sessions, the 100m. The table below shows the pattern of the repeat distances in these "long" sessions throughout thc build-up period.

INTERVAL DISTANCES OF 10 KILOMETER SESSIONS

WEEK	TUESDAY	THURSDAY	SATURDAY
1	500	1500	100
2	400	1000	100
3	200	3000	100
4	800	2000	100
5	600	1200	100
6	500	1500	100
7	400	1000	100
8	200	3000	100
9	800	2000	100
10	600	1200	—

Wednesday is a recovery day, after Tuesday's strenuous efforts and before Thursday's next "long" session. The 50m distances included in the Wednesday morning session are not sprints. They are there as technique swims. A lot of time should be spent on drilling the rate and size of a swimmer's stroke. Good swimmers should be able to swim any asked for number of strokes to a 25m or 50m length. It is a skill that must be automatic and accurate. It is a fundamental measure of the swimmer's control over their trade. The 50m distances are included in order that swimmers can hone this skill. Experiment by asking the swimmer to complete lengths in different numbers of strokes. Very soon they will begin to take great pride in their ability to control their swimming to exactly the number and effort of strokes required. It is worthwhile stressing again that in the recovery swims it is important swimmers observe the meaning of the word recovery – take it easy. Don't feel you're doing even better by going hard in a recovery session. Progress is a matter of stress followed by recovery. Short change either and your results will suffer.

Thursday's training involves a kick session in the morning and the week's second "long" session in the afternoon. Much of the kick training in the build-up is done using fins. Fins are a valuable tool for strengthening a swimmer's kick, especially their ankles. In this respect fins contribute even to breaststroke where strong ankles add greatly to the final snap of the breaststroke kick. Swimmers should not purchase the small, trendy fins so admired in some swim squads. If you are going to kick with fins that small, you might as well save yourself the money and kick with bare feet. Buy the medium size fins, the ones that have a fin around 40cms long and are usually the cheapest in the shop. A pair of fins should last one 1000km build-up. Their life expectancy can be extended by taping the foot portion of the fin with elastic electrician's tape.

No one coached by me has ever used a pull buoy. The swimming shown in these schedules, as pull should be done just with hand paddles or with hand paddles and ankles strapped together. Pull buoys make swimming easier when the purpose of doing pull is to make swimming harder. Even worse, pull buoys actually encourage a lazy body position. Lifting their hips up, in every stroke, is something swimmers must do for themselves, not lie on a hunk of polystyrene. I once saw a squad doing pull with both hand paddles and fins. Now that really is crazy. The two accessories contradict each other. So when you are swimming pull, use your hand paddles, maybe tie your ankles together but throw your pull buoy out and leave your fins on the pool deck.

Weights on Friday this week are the first session of the third cycle. Having increased the weights lifted by one increment in the second cycle, I usually do not increase the weight again in this third cycle. The next four sessions consolidate the heavier weights lifted in the second cycle. In the weight program, the same exercise, pull down front, appears to be repeated twice. This is not the case. In session two, the bar should be held with an over-the-top-of-the-bar grip. In session three this should change to an under-the-bar grip. The change sounds small but it changes completely the muscle groups exercised.

YOUNGER AND LESS EXPERIENCED SWIMMERS

Swimming training in the "pre-Lydiard" early years should also involve more diversity each day or each week than is characteristic of the Lydiard program. Time should be spent on starts, turns, steady swims, short sprints, drills, stroke correction and kick. The important and defining characteristic of swimming in these years is diversity – constructive play. Young swimmers benefit from being subject to a wide range of swimming experiences. Water skill drills such as otter and rock-n-roll are important. Otter involves diving to the bottom of the pool coming up, rolling over before diving back to the bottom again. Rock-n-roll is swimming down the pool doing one stroke backstroke followed by one stroke freestyle. Don't be afraid to set some longer swims. I've seen young squads do up to 3000m straight swims. They usually love complaining about it and then travel home telling their parents how great they are. The straight swims are very valuable. They begin establishing the physiological and psychological foundation necessary to tackle the full Lydiard program.

WEEK THREE SCHEDULES

Week Three – Monday AM – 6000 Mixed				
Warm-up	1000	Kick, With Fins Your Choice		
Swim	5 x 200	Done As		1) Butterfly 2) Backstroke 3) Breaststroke 4) Freestyle 5) Individual Medley
Kick	1000	Kick, With Fins Your Choice		
Swim	10 x 100	Butterfly		
Kick	1000	Done As	200 800	Breaststroke No Fins Your Choice
Swim	20 x 50	Done As	5 x 50 Each Stroke	

Week Three – Monday PM – 8000 Individual Medley	
Set One – No Fins 1000 Backstroke Swim 700 Freestyle Swim 200 Breaststroke Swim 100 Breaststroke Kick	Set Two – With Fins 1000 Butterfly / Butterfly Drills, Your Choice Of Mix 700 Freestyle Kick 200 Backstroke Kick 100 Butterfly Kick
Set Three – No Fins 1000 Backstroke Pull 700 Freestyle Pull 200 Breaststroke Swim 100 Breaststroke Kick	Set Four – With Fins 1000 Individual Medley, Done As 1x400, 1x200, 1x400 Individual Medley 700 Freestyle Kick 200 Backstroke Kick 100 Butterfly Kick

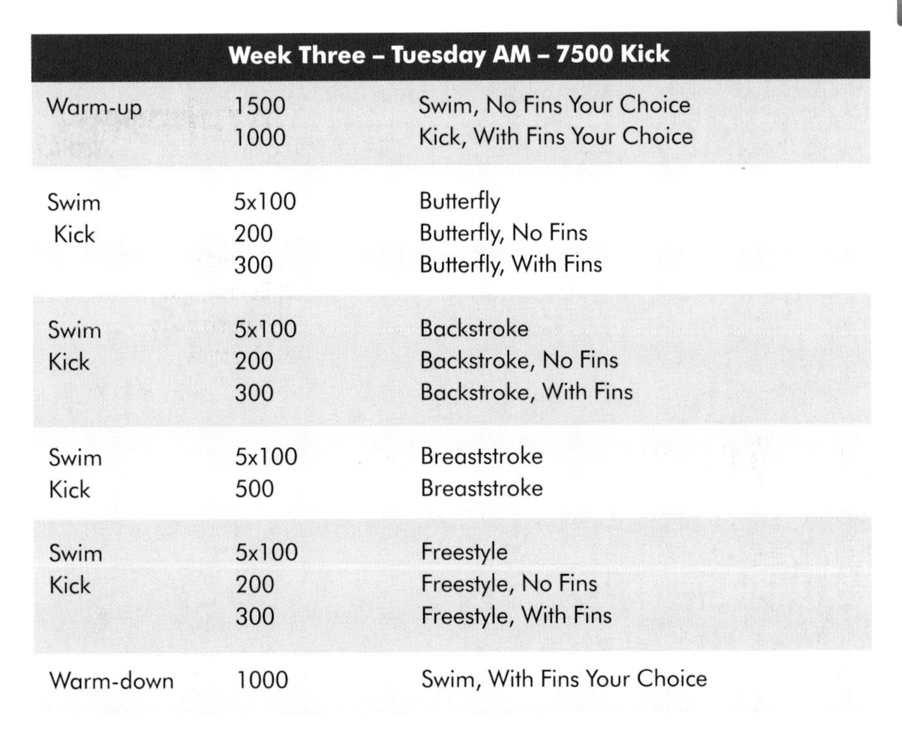

Week Three – Tuesday AM – 7500 Kick		
Warm-up	1500	Swim, No Fins Your Choice
	1000	Kick, With Fins Your Choice
Swim	5x100	Butterfly
Kick	200	Butterfly, No Fins
	300	Butterfly, With Fins
Swim	5x100	Backstroke
Kick	200	Backstroke, No Fins
	300	Backstroke, With Fins
Swim	5x100	Breaststroke
Kick	500	Breaststroke
Swim	5x100	Freestyle
Kick	200	Freestyle, No Fins
	300	Freestyle, With Fins
Warm-down	1000	Swim, With Fins Your Choice

Week Three – Tuesday PM – 10,000 Long		
Warm-up	1000	Kick, With Fins Your Choice
	1000	Swim, No Fins Your Choice
Main Set	10x200	Freestyle Swim
	8x200	Freestyle Pull
	4x200	Breaststroke Swim
	4x200	Backstroke Swim
	4x200	Backstroke Pull
Warm-down	1000	Kick, With Fins Your Choice
	1000	Swim, With Fins Your Choice

Week Three – Tuesday – Weights

Session Three

- Pull Down Front
- Dips
- Dumb Bell Behind Head
- Machine Pull Together
- Tricep Push Downs
- Leg Raises
- 15min. Bike

Week Three – Wednesday AM – 8000 Mixed		
Warm-up	1000	Kick, With Fins Your Choice
	1000	Swim, No Fins Your Choice
	1000	Pull, No Fins Your Choice
Main Set	16x200	Individual Medley
Warm-down	1000	Kick, With Fins Your Choice
	800	Swim, With Fins Your Choice

Week Three – Wednesday PM – 6000 Mixed		
Warm-up	500	Kick, With Fins Your Choice
	500	Swim, No Fins Your Choice
	500	Pull, No Fins Your Choice
Main Set	1500	Butterfly/ Butterfly Drills Your Choice
	1500	Backstroke, Pull
Warm-down	1000	Kick, With Fins Your Choice
	500	Swim, With Fins Your Choice

Week Three – Wednesday – Weights

Session Four

- Seated Rows
- Bench Press
- Bend Over Rows
- Machine Push Aparts
- Cleans
- Hamstrings
- 15min. Bike

Week Three – Thursday AM – 7500 Kick

Warm-up	1500	Swim, No Fins Your Choice
	1500	Pull, No Fins Your Choice
Main Set	3000	Kick, With Fins Your Choice
	500	Kick, No Fins, Min.100 Breaststroke
Warm-down	1000	Swim, With Fins Your Choice

Week Three – Thursday PM – 10,000 Long

Warm-up	1000	Kick, With Fins Your Choice
	1000	Swim, No Fins Your Choice
Main Set	1x3000	Swim, Freestyle
	1x3000	Pull, Freestyle
Warm-down	1000	Kick, With Fins Your Choice
	1000	Swim, With Fins Your Choice

Week Three – Thursday – Weights

Session One

- Pull Down Behind
- Chin Ups
- Flies
- Wrist Curls
- Forearm Pull Downs
- Sit Ups
- 15min. Bike

Week Three – Friday AM – 6000 Mixed

Swim	1000	No Fins Your Choice
Kick	1500	With Fins Your Choice
Pull	1000	No Fins Your Choice
Swim	1000	Individual Medley, With Fins Your Choice Done As 100 Butterfly 200 Individual Medley 100 Backstroke 200 Individual Medley 100 Breaststroke 200 Individual Medley 100 Freestyle
Kick	1500	With Fins Your Choice

Week Three – Friday PM – 8000 Medley

Set One	2000	Swim, Freestyle, No Fins
	1200	Kick, Freestyle, With Fins
	800	Pull, Freestyle, No Fins
Set Two	1400	Swim, Backstroke, No Fins
	800	Kick, Backstroke, With Fins
	400	Pull, Backstroke, No Fins
Set Three	800	Swim, Individual Medley, No Fins
	400	Kick, Individual Medley, With Fins Except Breaststroke
	200	Swim, Individual Medley, No Fins

Week Three – Friday – Weights

Session Two

- Pull Down Front
- Curls
- Elbow Raises
- Two Form Dips
- Back Lifts
- Squats
- 15min. Bike

Week Three – Saturday AM – 10,000 Waitakeres

Warm-up	1000	Kick, With Fins Your Choice
Swim/Pull	20x100	Freestyle, Done As 10xSwim, 10xPull
Kick	1000	Kick, With Fins Your Choice
Swim/Pull	20x100	Backstroke,10xSwim, 10xPull
Kick	1000	Kick, With Fins Your Choice
Swim	20x100	Individual Medley, Swim
Warm-down	1000	Swim, With Fins Your Choice

Week Three – Saturday PM – 5000 Kick

Warm-up	1000 1000	Kick, With Fins Your Choice Swim, No Fins Your Choice	
Drills	500		
Stroke Correction	800		
Kick	3x400	With Fins,	1) Freestyle 2) Backstroke 3) Butterfly
Kick	500	Breaststroke	

Week Three – Sunday AM – 8000 Mixed		
Warm-up	2000	No Fins Your Choice
Swim	20x50	Freestyle, No Fins
Kick	2000	With Fins Your Choice
Swim	20x50	Breaststroke
Pull	2000	No Fins Your Choice

Week Three – Sunday – Weights

Session Three

- Pull Down Front
- Dips
- Dumb Bell Behind Head
- Machine Pull Together
- Tricep Push Downs
- Leg Raises
- 15min. Bike

NOTES TO WEEK THREE SCHEDULES

You will have noticed by now that the build-up includes quite a bit of medley swimming. Medleys are a valuable aid to achieving well-rounded conditioning, irrespective of the athlete's competitive specialty. To quote the Australian, New South Wales, Swimming Almanac, medleys promote "skill development in all four strokes, encourage overall muscle development, give swimmers more options in their swimming careers and teach new skills and drills." They are a foundation from which great things can accrue.

Hand over back *Probably the world's most common drill.*

Thursday morning's training emphasizes kick. The 3000m straight kick provides leg muscles with the same general aerobic conditioning that swimming provides the shoulders, arms and back. Do not neglect good leg conditioning. Race results will be seriously affected if swimmer's legs are unable to maintain the race rhythm throughout the event.

Thumbs up free *Emphasizes the importance of shoulders and back.*

Thursday afternoon's program is a further "long" 10km session. Recording the times taken for these swims means the results can be compared with the same swim in the second five weeks of the build-up and allows progress to be measured season by season. If proof of the validity of the Lydiard conditioning program was ever needed, it is in the improvement swimmers will see in the speed of these swims. It is worthwhile emphasizing again that these swims must not be swum anaerobically. Proper conditioning requires they are swum as firm aerobic efforts. The swimmer's heart rate should be kept in the range of 130-150bpm and certainly held below 160bpm. Do not, however, become a heart rate monitor slave. In time, swimmers intuitively know how to swim at a speed where the effort is high, but is still contributing to their aerobic fitness, not using it up.

Janet Evans *Quickly improves the size of a swimmer's stroke.*

In our first book "Swim to the Top", a table of Jane Copland's times is shown. The table compares the times Jane swam for various aerobic "long" swims from the season she began training through to the season she broke her first New Zealand Open Record. Shown in the table below are some sample times taken from that table.

Bounding *A sprinter's drill.*

JANE COPLAND – AEROBIC SWIM TIMES

Distance	First Season Best Average Time	Final Season Best Average Time
500	6.21.92	5.40.30
1000	13.00.00	11.49.00
400	5.12.00	4.41.65
200	2.35.80	2.18.77
1500	20.09.45	17.54.00
3000	38.49.00	36.28.00*

*This time is a current time and different from that in "Swim to the Top".

Fists *Teaches the correct underwater pull pattern.*

You can see that although the swims are aerobic they are not exactly slow. Lydiard is often credited with being the father of the "long slow distance method" of training. He was not. Just try and swim 2 x 3000m in 36.28.00 for each 3000m. That's not slow. And yet to a well-conditioned swimmer it is still an aerobic effort. For anaerobically over-trained athletes, swims such as these would be impossible aerobically and maybe anaerobically as well. In this principle lies the reason our runners can't get anywhere near the African athletes. It's called aerobic conditioning. You get it by long, fast aerobic effort over many, many miles. Hold on to that idea, it might make you a world record holder one day.

One final irony on the same subject is the number of times coaches, parents and swimmers from anaerobic programs have slated our aerobic training by trotting out lines such as, "If you want to race fast you have to train fast" or

"The only thing swimming 100kms does is make you good at swimming 100kms" or even better, quote Nike at you with, "Go hard or go home." What they ignore or just don't understand is that aerobically well-conditioned swimmers are often training at higher speeds aerobically than their swimmers can anaerobically. They are just not killing themselves doing it.

Drag *Emphasizes the shoulder movement so important to good freestyle.*

Saturday's training consists of a normal session of "100m" in the morning and the stroke correction session in the afternoon. Even during the build-up the stroke correction session each week includes a set of drills. The table below lists the drills making up the 500m set. They should be swum in this order and as 25m of each drill. A full explanation of these drills is included in "Swim to the Top".

STROKE DRILLS

FREESTYLE	BREASTSTROKE
1. Hand Over Back	13. Three Kick Breaststroke
2. Thumbs Up	14. Breast Arms, Fly Kick
3. Janet Evans	15. Delayed Kick Breaststroke
4. Four Plus Four	16. Distance per Stroke (DPS)
5. Drag	
6. Bounding	
7. Fists	
8. Distance per Stroke (DPS)	
BACKSTROKE	**BUTTERFLY**
9. Three Second Backstroke	17. Fly Drills
10. Thumbs Up Backstroke	18. Distance per Stroke (DPS)
11. Double Arm Backstroke	19. Fly Drills
12. Distance per Stroke (DPS)	20. Normal Butterfly

Double Arm Backstroke *The best drill to teach the bent arm backstroke pull.*

Thumbs Up Backstroke *Teaches that good shoulder movement is important in backstroke.*

Fly Drills *A good drill for teaching distance per stroke in butterfly.*

Done this way, the drills form a mini stroke correction lesson. If the drills have been taught properly and the swimmer knows the reason for doing each drill, the very process of swimming one length of each drill reminds the athlete of the important elements of all four strokes. If a swimmer discovers a new drill that emphasizes something important, then it should be added to the drill routine. Two drills to stay clear of are One Arm Freestyle and Catch-up. One Arm Freestyle always has the swimmer lifting their right shoulder when the right arm is pulling and the left shoulder when the left arm is pulling. What should happen is exactly the opposite. One Arm Freestyle is teaching something that is wrong so don't use it. Catch-up freestyle used to be very popular until Popov, de Bruin and one or two other not too bad scholars of the freestyle trade discovered that alternating freestyle, which is where the arms pull and recover 180 degrees apart, is faster. It is better not to use a drill that is out of date.

Some caution should be exercised when copying other people's drills. When I was coaching Toni Jeffs, we shared a pool with another coach who instructed a band of keen young 10-12 year olds. When we came back from an overseas visit with a new drill, within a week the other coach would have her squad doing the same drill. Nothing wrong with that – it's the way learning takes place. However just for fun, Toni Jeffs and I decided to try an experiment. For a week Toni included, in her normal routine, 25m of a drill that was just a silly invention. It had no swimming merit whatsoever. It involved Toni swimming freestyle and kicking her foot high in the air and reaching back and slapping the sole of her foot with her hand. You needed to be as good as Toni just to do the drill. Within a week though, the keen young 10-12 year

olds were all over the pool trying to master the new drill. So, copy drills by all means but know what they're for before inflicting them on some poor soul in a swimming pool.

YOUNGER AND LESS EXPERIENCED SWIMMERS

Introducing young swimmers to a Lydiard conditioning program is a daunting prospect for both coach and swimmer. It needs to be approached recognizing that additional mileage can only be introduced at a pace each swimmer can handle. That's true of course even for older athletes swimming this program for the first time. The problem is there is no rule. Some young people seem to be able to absorb the work involved in swimming these distances quite quickly. A few might never make it. Whatever the pace of progress, the coach needs to handle this period with patience. An important and fundamental change is being made in the level of commitment expected from the young swimmer. It involves very big mental and physical demands. A little patience in making sure the process is not rushed is important.

DPS Fly *As with all strokes distance per stroke is vital to good butterfly.*

Breaststroke with Fly Kick
Teaches the undulating push of good modern breaststroke.

WEEK FOUR SCHEDULES

Week Four – Monday AM – 6000 Mixed				
Warm-up	1000	Kick, With Fins Your Choice		
Swim	5 x 200	Done As		1) Butterfly 2) Backstroke 3) Breaststroke 4) Freestyle 5) Individual Medley
Kick	1000	Kick, With Fins Your Choice		
Swim	10 x 100	Freestyle		
Kick	1000	Done As	200 800	Breaststroke With Fins Your Choice
Swim	20 x 50	Done As	5 x 50	Each Stroke

Week Four – Monday PM – 8000 Individual Medley

Set One – No Fins
2000 Freestyle Swim

Set Two – With Fins
1000 Butterfly / Butterfly Drills, Your Choice Of Mix
500 Freestyle Kick
300 Backstroke Kick
200 Butterfly Kick

Set Three – No Fins
2000 Backstroke Pull

Set Four – With Fins
1000 Individual Medley
500 Freestyle Kick
300 Backstroke Kick
200 Butterfly Kick

Week Four – Tuesday AM – 7500 Kick		
Warm-up	2000	Swim, No Fins Your Choice
Kick	9x300	With Fins, Done As 1) Freestyle 2) Backstroke, Freestyle, Butterfly x 100 3) Freestyle 4) Backstroke 5) Backstroke, Freestyle, Butterfly x 100 6) Backstroke 7) Butterfly 8) Backstroke, Freestyle, Butterfly x 100 9) Butterfly
Swim, Kick, Drill	8x100	No Fins, Done As 1) Breaststroke 2) Breaststroke 3) Delayed Breaststroke 4) Breaststroke Kick 5) Breaststroke 6) Breaststroke 7) Delayed Breaststroke 8) Breaststroke Kick
Warm-down	1000 1000	Kick, With Fins Your Choice Swim, With Fins Your Choice

Week Four – Tuesday PM – 10,000 Long		
Warm-up	1000 1000	Kick, With Fins Your Choice Swim, No Fins Your Choice
Main Set	3x800 2x800	Freestyle Swim Freestyle Pull
	1x400	Individual Medley Swim
	1x800 1x800	Backstroke Swim Backstroke Pull
Warm-down	1000 1000	Kick, With Fins Your Choice Swim, With Fins Your Choice

Week Four – Tuesday – Weights

Session Four

- Seated Rows
- Bench Press
- Bend Over Rows
- Machine Push Aparts
- Cleans
- Hamstrings
- 15min. Bike

Week Four – Wednesday AM – 8000 Mixed

Warm-up	1500	Kick, With Fins Your Choice
	1500	Swim, No Fins Your Choice
Swim	20x50	Butterfly
Main Set	4x100	Individual Medley
	500	Kick, No Fins, Min.100 Breaststroke
	4x50	Breaststroke
	500	Kick, No Fins, Min.100 Breaststroke
	4x100	Breaststroke
Swim	20x50	Backstroke
Warm-down	500	Kick, With Fins Your Choice
	500	Swim, With Fins Your Choice

Week Four – Wednesday PM – 6000 Mixed

Warm-up	500	Kick, With Fins Your Choice
	500	Swim, No Fins Your Choice
	500	Pull, No Fins Your Choice
Main Set	1500	Breaststroke, With Fins, Butterfly Kick
	1500	Freestyle, Pull, No Fins
Warm-down	1000	Kick, With Fins Your Choice
	500	Swim, With Fins Your Choice

Week Four – Wednesday – Weights

Session One

- Pull Down Behind
- Chin Ups
- Flies
- Wrist Curls
- Forearm Pull Downs
- Sit Ups
- 15min. Bike

Week Four – Thursday AM – 7500 Kick

Warm-up	1500	Swim, No Fins Your Choice	
	1500	Pull, No Fins Your Choice	
Main Set	4x300	Kick, Each 300 Done As	100 Freestyle
			100 Backstroke
			100 Butterfly
	6x300	Kick, Done As	1) 300 Freestyle
			2) 300 Backstroke
			3) 300 Butterfly
			4) 300 Freestyle
			5) 300 Backstroke
			6) 300 Butterfly
	500	Kick, No Fins, Min.100 Breaststroke	
Warm-down	1000	Swim, With Fins Your Choice	

Week Four – Thursday PM – 10,000 Long

Warm-up	1000	Kick, With Fins Your Choice
	1000	Swim, No Fins Your Choice
Main Set	1x2000	Swim, Freestyle
	1x2000	Pull, Freestyle
	1x2000	Swim, Backstroke
Warm-down	1000	Kick, With Fins Your Choice
	1000	Swim, With Fins Your Choice

Week Four – Thursday – Weights

Session Two

- Pull Down Front
- Curls
- Elbow Raises
- Two Form Dips
- Back Lifts
- Squats
- 15min. Bike

Week Four – Friday AM – 6000 Mixed		
Swim	1000	No Fins Your Choice
Kick	1500	With Fins Your Choice
Pull	1000	No Fins Your Choice
Swim	1000	Individual Medley, With Fins Your Choice Done As 100 Butterfly 200 Individual Medley 100 Backstroke 200 Individual Medley 100 Breaststroke 200 Individual Medley 100 Freestyle
Kick	1500	With Fins Your Choice

Week Four – Friday PM – 8000 Medley		
Set One	4x1000	1) Swim, Freestyle, No Fins 2) Swim, Backstroke, No Fins 3) Pull, Freestyle, No Fins 4) Pull, Backstroke, No Fins
Set Two	4x700	1) Kick, Freestyle, With Fins 2) Kick, Backstroke, With Fins 3) Kick, Butterfly, With Fins 4) Kick, Freestyle, With Fins
Set Three	4x200	Swim, Individual Medley, No Fins
Set Four	4x100	Swim, Breaststroke, No Fins

Week Four – Friday – Weights

Session Three

- Pull Down Front
- Dips
- Dumb Bell Behind Head
- Machine Pull Together
- Tricep Push Downs
- Leg Raises
- 15min. Bike

Week Four – Saturday AM – 10,000 Waitakeres		
Warm-up	1500 1500	Swim, No Fins Your Choice Kick, With Fins Your Choice
Main Set	20x100	Freestyle, 10xSwim, 10xPull
Swim/Kick	1500 1500	Swim, No Fins Your Choice Kick, With Fins Your Choice
Main Set	20x100	Done As 10xBackstroke,(5xSwim,5xPull) 10xIndividual Medley

Week Four – Saturday PM – 5000 Kick			
Warm-up	1000 1000	Kick, With Fins Your Choice Swim, No Fins Your Choice	
Drills	500		
Stroke Correction	800		
Kick	3x400	With Fins,	1) Freestyle 2) Backstroke 3) Butterfly
Kick	500	Breaststroke	

Week Four – Sunday AM – 8000 Mixed		
Warm-up	2000	No Fins Your Choice
Swim	20x50	Butterfly , No Fins
Kick	2000	With Fins Your Choice
Swim	20x50	Backstroke, No Fins
Pull	2000	No Fins Your Choice

Week Four – Sunday – Weights

Session Four

- Seated Rows
- Bench Press
- Bend Over Rows
- Machine Push Aparts
- Cleans
- Hamstrings
- 15min. Bike

NOTES TO WEEK FOUR SCHEDULES

It may have been noticed by now that a number of schedules are the same or close to the same each week. I make no apology for this. Far too much effort in swimming goes into inventing different schedules just for the sake of having a different schedule. I am aware of a number of coaches who take great pride in never having set the same schedule twice. However, if a schedule is ideal for recovery or stroke correction or aerobic conditioning then why not repeat it through the build-up. It is, after all, only ten weeks and if a top athlete can't do the same schedule ten times each six months then he or she doesn't deserve to be an even better athlete. Jane Copland has got to the stage where she can tell you the schedule to be swum every day throughout the ten weeks. Far from being boring, this knowledge provides swimmers with a sense of certainty. They know what's expected and can get on with the task of doing it. My attitude towards this question is colored by the years spent coaching runners. True, runners do have the variety of the wide outdoors but many of them run the same ten-mile course day after day week after week without appearing to suffer. The point is, if you have a good schedule for some purpose, stick to it. Good swimmers won't mind at all.

Monday afternoon's training includes a 1000m butterfly. Long butterfly swims need to be swum with caution. The butterfly technique can very quickly deteriorate when the stroke is swum for any great distance. Tiredness can cause the legs and hips to sink and the whole thing becomes most depressing indeed. When this happens there is no point in continuing the swim. Don't practice something that is clearly wrong. Fitting in two or three lengths of fly drills can however continue the swim. Once the swimmer has recovered, full butterfly can begin again.

One aspect of breaststroke training included in these programs deserves special mention. The kick is a most important part of the breaststroke. When it is being swum in training, a lot of attention should be paid to the distance per kick. A good female breaststroke swimmer should be able to kick 25m in five kicks and drop that still further by holding the glide.

A key feature of the modern breaststroke kick is a strong upsweep of the swimmer's feet as they come together at the end of each kick. This powerful upsweep should be practiced constantly. It is an indispensable ingredient of good breaststroke swimming. Anyone doubting this should look at the underwater shots of Kovacs, Poewe and Kowal at the Sydney Olympic Games. They are all good at it. Kovacs is the best, but I guess she should be; she did win the race. The key point is that there is a strong upsweep, but no downward kick. That means the kick is legal. The rules say no downward dolphin kick is permitted and there isn't any. Unfortunately, many New Zealand officials are years behind the rest of the world and haven't realized that at the end of a breaststroke kick the feet can sweep up without kicking down. Jane Copland was disqualified in Auckland for this by a referee who clearly had no idea what he was on about. At a National Swimming Championships held shortly after that, a group of officials sneaked down to the underwater viewing windows to inspect just Jane's new, for New Zealand, kick. Fortunately I was good mates with one of the pool attendants who told me the officials were under the pool trying to find something in the kick to disqualify Jane. I went to the Meet Director who had been leading the posse and said,"What's going on?" She looked like she'd been caught with her hand in the cash till, which, in a manner of speaking I suppose she had. It never happened again.

One of the disadvantages of living in a small, relatively isolated country like New Zealand is the lack of exposure many aspects of life get to the educating influences of the outside world and swimming officials are no exception. Since she was twelve years old, Jane Copland has swum 430 races. Almost exactly half (212) have been swum overseas in a combined total of 50 visits to 16 different countries. The balance of 218 have been swum in New Zealand. Overseas she has been disqualified once and in New Zealand ten times. Now the one thing you could bet the house on is that her swimming did not change. Her breaststroke in Imperia, Italy was exactly the same as in Napier, New Zealand. Why, then was she 1000% more likely to be disqualified in Napier than in Imperia? New Zealand's officials would probably claim it was because Italian officials let their swimmers get away with blue murder. I don't believe that's true. I believe the attitude and the knowledge of swimming, of New Zealand officials is poor. The attitudes of the majority exhibit the liberal leanings of a Tianimun Square traffic cop.

The principle step required to correct this is to educate New Zealand officials that their task is not to search for errors in the best traditions of a police state, but to facilitate the smooth conduct of a race, a swim meet and a sport. Australian officials are very good at this. They say a sport gets the athletes it deserves. The Australians have and so have we.

YOUNGER AND LESS EXPERIENCED SWIMMERS

Although patience is the key to successfully introducing young swimmers to Lydiard type conditioning I have frequently been amazed by the resilience of young people. One squad I coached in the United States, Virgin Islands took just four months to move from a traditional 25 kilometers a week interval program to 100 kilometers per week Lydiard type conditioning. These were experienced swimmers of 16 and 17. Nevertheless, it does show how quickly the transition can be made. The table below shows the weekly distance swum by three of these swimmers in their first build-up and after just four months. It should be noted that Branden was only 13 years old when he swam these distances.

Week	1	2	3	4	5	6	7	8	9	10
Kerri	36	94	92	100	96	85	84	90	92	96
Nicole	97	100	98	100	100	95	92	95	100	95
Branden	91	90	92	90	91	92	90	65	60	75

Younger swimmers of 11 or 12 years of age, making the change from the junior squads, will take longer than the squad in the Virgin Islands. As a rule of thumb, I expect the process to take about two years. In other words, a 12 year old leaving the junior squad would normally be capable of swimming the full Lydiard program in this book by the age of 14. Jane Copland made the transition quite quickly. She began when she was 12 and swam her first week of 100 kilometers when she was 13. She managed her first four or five consecutive weeks when she was 14.

WEEK FIVE SCHEDULES

Week Five – Monday AM – 6000 Mixed				
Warm-up	1000	Kick, With Fins Your Choice		
Swim	5 x 200	Done As		1) Butterfly 2) Backstroke 3) Breaststroke 4) Freestyle 5) Individual Medley
Kick	1000	Kick, With Fins Your Choice		
Swim	10 x 100	Backstroke		
Kick	1000	Done As	200 800	Breaststroke No Fins Your Choice
Swim	0 x 50	Done As	5 x 50	Each Stroke

Week Five – Monday PM – 8000 Individual Medley

Set One – No Fins
1000 Freestyle Swim
700 Backstroke Swim
200 Breaststroke Swim
100 Breaststroke Kick

Set Two – With Fins
1000 Butterfly / Butterfly Drills, Your Choice Of Mix
700 Freestyle Kick
200 Backstroke Kick
100 Butterfly Kick

Set Three – No Fins
1000 Freestyle Pull
700 Backstroke Pull
200 Breaststroke Swim
100 Breaststroke Kick

Set Four – With Fins
1000 Individual Medley, Done As 1x400, 1x200, 1x400 Individual Medley
700 Freestyle Kick
200 Backstroke Kick
100 Butterfly Kick

Week Five – Tuesday AM – 7500 Kick		
Warm-up	1500	Swim, No Fins Your Choice
	1000	Kick, With Fins Your Choice
Swim	5x100	Butterfly
Kick	200	Butterfly, No Fins
	300	Butterfly, With Fins
Swim	5x100	Backstroke
Kick	200	Backstroke, No Fins
	300	Backstroke, With Fins
Swim	5x100	Breaststroke
Kick	500	Breaststroke
Swim	5x100	Freestyle
Kick	200	Freestyle, No Fins
	300	Freestyle, With Fins
Warm-down	1000	Swim, With Fins Your Choice

Week Five – Tuesday PM – 10,000 Long		
Warm-up	1000	Kick, With Fins Your Choice
	1000	Swim, No Fins Your Choice
Main Set	3x600	Freestyle Swim
	2x600	Freestyle Pull
	1x600	Individual Medley Swim
	2x600	Backstroke Swim
	2x600	Backstroke Pull
Warm-down	1000	Kick, With Fins Your Choice
	1000	Swim, With Fins Your Choice

Week Five – Tuesday – Weights

Session One

- Pull Down Behind
- Chin Ups
- Flies
- Wrist Curls
- Forearm Pull Downs
- Sit Ups
- 15min. Bike

Week Five – Wednesday AM – 8000 Mixed		
Warm-up	1000	Kick, With Fins Your Choice
	1000	Swim, No Fins Your Choice
	1000	Pull, No Fins Your Choice
Main Set	32x100	Individual Medley
Warm-down	1000	Kick, With Fins Your Choice
	800	Swim, With Fins Your Choice

Week Five – Wednesday PM – 6000 Mixed		
Warm-up	500	Kick, With Fins Your Choice
	500	Swim, No Fins Your Choice
	500	Pull, No Fins Your Choice
Main Set	1500	Butterfly/ Butterfly Drills Your Choice
	1500	Backstroke, Pull
Warm-down	1000	Kick, With Fins Your Choice
	500	Swim, With Fins Your Choice

Week Five – Wednesday – Weights

Session Two

- Pull Down Front
- Curls
- Elbow Raises
- Two Form Dips
- Back Lifts
- Squats
- 15min. Bike

Week Five – Thursday AM – 7500 Kick		
Warm-up	1500	Swim, No Fins Your Choice
	1500	Pull, No Fins Your Choice
Main Set	3000	Kick, With Fins Your Choice
	500	Kick, No Fins, Min.100 Breaststroke
Warm-down	1000	Swim, With Fins Your Choice

Week Five – Thursday PM – 10,000 Long		
Warm-up	1000	Kick, With Fins Your Choice
	1000	Swim, No Fins Your Choice
Main Set	2x1200	Swim, Freestyle
	1x1200	Pull, Freestyle
	1x1200	Swim, Backstroke
	1x1200	Pull, Backstroke
Warm-down	1000	Kick, With Fins Your Choice
	1000	Swim, With Fins Your Choice

Week Five – Thursday – Weights

Session Three

- Pull Down Front
- Dips
- Dumb Bell Behind Head
- Machine Pull Together
- Tricep Push Downs
- Leg Raises
- 15min. Bike

Week Five – Friday AM – 6000 Mixed

Swim	1000	No Fins Your Choice	
Kick	1500	With Fins Your Choice	
Pull	1000	No Fins Your Choice	
Swim	1000	Individual Medley, With Fins Your Choice	
		Done As	100 Butterfly
			200 Individual Medley
			100 Backstroke
			200 Individual Medley
			100 Breaststroke
			200 Individual Medley
			100 Freestyle
Kick	1500	With Fins Your Choice	

Week Five – Friday PM – 8000 Medley

Set One	2000	Swim, Freestyle, No Fins
	1200	Kick, Freestyle, With Fins
	800	Pull, Freestyle, No Fins
Set Two	1400	Swim, Backstroke, No Fins
	800	Kick, Backstroke, With Fins
	400	Pull, Backstroke, No Fins
Set Three	800	Swim, Individual Medley
	400	Kick, Individual Medley
	200	Swim, Individual Medley

Week Five – Friday – Weights

Session Four

- Seated Rows
- Bench Press
- Bend Over Rows
- Machine Push Aparts
- Cleans
- Hamstrings
- 15min. Bike

Week Five – Saturday AM – 10,000 Waitakeres

Swim	100x100	Freestyle, 15 sec. Rest Between Each 100

Week Five – Saturday PM – 5000 Kick

Warm-up	1000 1000	Kick, With Fins Your Choice Swim, No Fins Your Choice	
Drills	500		
Stroke Correction	800		
Kick	3x400	With Fins	1) Freestyle 2) Backstroke 3) Butterfly
Kick	500	Breaststroke	

Week Five – Sunday AM – 8000 Mixed

Warm-up	2000	No Fins Your Choice
Swim	20x50	Freestyle, No Fins
Kick	2000	With Fins Your Choice
Swim	20x50	Breaststroke
Pull	2000	No Fins Your Choice

Week Five – Sunday – Weights

Session One

- Pull Down Behind
- Chin Ups
- Flies
- Wrist Curls
- Forearm Pull Downs
- Sit Ups
- 15min. Bike

NOTES TO WEEK FIVE SCHEDULES

You have just completed half the build-up. It hasn't been that bad. The weeks are getting easier; the soreness is not quite as great. You still don't feel like an all night party, but at least you now feel you can finish the ten weeks. There will be some bad moments in the next five weeks, but generally the second half will be easier. In fact there will be fantastic moments when you start swimming and feel you can go faster and faster, further and further with no need to stop, with no chance of ever getting tired. It's almost an out of body experience, "Who is this swimming this fast? It can't be me. It is me. Amazing!" At that moment – and it will happen, it always does – you will have joined the clan known as Lydiard trained athletes. You will know for certain the training works. You will know you are going to race faster than you ever have before. No question.

On Saturday you will swim the first 100x100m with 15 seconds rest. It is a long and very tough session and yet as it gets easier and you get faster it begins to stand out as a benchmark of the improvement in your aerobic condition. The table opposite shows the progress in Jane Copland's 100x100m times since she was 12 years old through to when she was 17 and broke her first New Zealand open women's breaststroke record. Jane's improvement is shown not because it represents the final word in freestyle swimming but because it does demonstrate the progress in aerobic conditioning that will occur by following a Lydiard training program.

Cycling *Branden demonstrates cycling. I now have swimmers end every dry land session with 15 minutes of cycling. It's a good aerobic exercise and very good for swimmer's legs.*

JANE COPLAND – WAITAKERES TIMES

YEAR	AGE	100 X 100m AVERAGE TIME	PERCENTAGE IMPROVEMENT
1	12	1.17.60	-
2	13	1.16.70	1.2
3	14	1.14.19	3.3
4	15	1.10.19	5.4
5	16	1.09.12	1.5
6	17	1.07.07	3.0

Jane's progress also highlights the early age at which long distance training can be undertaken. Research at the International Center for Aquatic Research in the USA reveals that "aerobic development is the first factor to reach full development at about 14 years" and that prior to this age "the primary energy system is endurance, with the prepubescent swimmer having very little anaerobic capacity. Therefore endurance training should begin early and reach a peak in training emphasis by age 14. This approach avoids training designed to highlight a factor not near full development (i.e. anaerobic characteristics) when no adaptation is possible in that system." So there you have it, aerobic conditioning not only does no harm to young swimmers, it is the only type of training from which immature athletes are physiologically capable of deriving any benefit. And yet we have always known this.

The stories of young Kenyan children running to and from school have been around for years. It doesn't seem to have hurt their competitive results. Why then do so many swimming coaches – with stop watches poised – insist on giving young

Leg Press *Keri demonstrates the leg press. Never neglect strengthening swimmer's legs.*

swimmers "short programs of lots of sprints because that long distance stuff is no good for them?" One New Zealand Regional Chairman, not known for his perspicacity, went as far as to use his 2001 Annual Report to moan about the dangers of swimmers who "train long hours." I tried and failed to get across the idea that it's not the hours, it's what you do in the hours that matters. No wonder the sport has such a high and young mortality rate as coaches thrash young swimmers with training aimed at achieving a physiologically impossible goal. At least with long conditioning training, young people have the physiological development to accept and benefit from the training. Let me leave the last word on this subject to the International Center for Aquatic Research, "Endurance-based training may be the single most important component of training throughout the entire career of the athlete."

Some of the weight training exercises included in our schedules may cause comment by gym personal trainers and supervisors. They will not understand that the weight program has been developed specifically for swimming. Here are the four comments our swimmers have had to deal with most frequently.

1. Don't do the Pull Down Behind exercise. It will cause injury.
For the normal gym member this is good advice. The exercise does cause high stress in the neck and upper back area. For a swimmer however strengthening this area is most important. Lat. Pull Downs whether in front or behind are important. Start off with light weights and increase them gradually as the muscles get stronger and you should avoid injury. Put it this way: Toni Jeffs, Nichola Chellingworth and Jane Copland combined have done this exercise 8980 times without injury. Obey the rules and you shouldn't have a problem.

2. Don't move your back in Elbow Raises
Swimmers doing this exercise should drop the weight down to floor level after each lift by twisting their back and then lift the weight by using both the back and arm muscles. For normal gym members this is a real no-no. It puts too much stress on the lower back and is an exercise normally just for the arms. For swimmers, however, the back twisting movement is most important for good freestyle and backstroke. The exercise is valuable for strengthening this movement.

Elbow Raises *Branden demonstrates Elbow Raises. Branden is 13 years old and shows that a cautious weight program even at this age increases strength and causes no harm.*

3. Women shouldn't do Chin Ups

It sounds like something out of the dark ages. You would be surprised how often the comment has been made. I know a coach who used to have his male swimmers do Chin Ups as part of their warm-up but insisted the female swimmers did something else. I asked why and he muttered something about having children. It's absolute rubbish of course. Nichola Chellingworth could happily do 21 Chin Ups with ten kilograms tied around her waist. Please don't say, "Ah, but she hasn't had children yet." I couldn't bear it.

Chin-ups *Branden demonstrates chin ups. A good exercise for testing swimmer's arm strength to body weight.*

4. The weights you are lifting are too heavy

This comment is usually aimed at female swimmers. They shouldn't have to put up with it. It's said because the majority of people do not realize the strength of top female swimmers. Many of the exercises are done with weights well in excess of their body weight. The reason for lifting heavy weights is based on the principle that endurance will be developed by swimming and strength by weights. Swimming is, after all, an exercise involving lots of repetitions of a light weight. Since she was twelve years old I estimate Jane Copland has done nine and three quarter million arm strokes, all repetitions of a light weight. If you want to build endurance stay in the pool. It's the best place to do it and it is swimming specific. If you want to build strength, go to a gym and lift heavy weights.

Breast weights *Keri demonstrates the breaststroke arm press exercise using a machine designed for exercising legs but ideal for the breaststroke press.*

YOUNGER AND LESS EXPERIENCED SWIMMERS

In the process of introducing a young swimmer to Lydiard type conditioning, it is important to understand the distinction between swimming one week of 100 kilometers and swimming consecutive weeks of this distance. Any crazy coach can flog his squad through one week of 100 kilometers – and at training camps and the like many do. We are not doing that. What we are about is building the reserves of conditioning that enable young swimmers to train 100 kilometers each week – week after week. And that is a very different thing. The benefit of Lydiard conditioning is not in the 100 kilometers. It is in the fact that the 100 kilometers has to be repeated for ten weeks. It is important for coach and swimmer to recognize that this is the conditioning goal.

Because getting through the distance is the young swimmers immediate priority, it is important to put speed to one side. Push for both distance and speed at this stage and you will probably ruin some young athlete's promising career. As the distance increases, the swimmer will get stronger and faster without the coach demanding personal best sets. While I'm writing this, Branden – he's the young 13 year old swimmer who began Lydiard type conditioning 20 weeks ago and is now swimming 93 kilometers each week – has come into my office and said, "It's strange 20 weeks ago I had trouble making 1.30 minutes for the Waitakeres 100s. Now I can hold 1.12 no problem." I have just told him," That's not strange at all. It's called getting aerobically fitter."

WEEK SIX SCHEDULES

Week Six – Monday AM – 6000 Mixed				
Warm-up	1000	Kick, With Fins Your Choice		
Swim	5 x 200	Done As		1) Butterfly 2) Backstroke 3) Breaststroke 4) Freestyle 5) Individual Medley
Kick	1000	Kick, With Fins Your Choice		
Swim	10 x 100	Butterfly		
Kick	1000	Done As	200 800	Breaststroke No Fins Your Choice
Swim	20 x 50	Done As	5 x 50	Each Stroke

Week Six – Monday PM – 8000 Individual Medley

Set One – No Fins
2000 Backstroke Swim

Set Two – With Fins
1000 Butterfly / Butterfly Drills, Your Choice Of Mix
500 Freestyle Kick
300 Backstroke Kick
200 Butterfly Kick

Set Three – No Fins
2000 Freestyle Pull

Set Four – With Fins
1000 Individual Medley, Done As 1x400, 1x200, 1x400 Individual Medley
500 Freestyle Kick
300 Backstroke Kick
200 Butterfly Kick

Week Six – Tuesday AM – 7500 Kick		
Warm-up	2000	Swim, No Fins Your Choice
Kick	9x300	With Fins, Done As 1) Freestyle 2) Backstroke, Freestyle, Butterfly x 100 3) Freestyle 4) Backstroke 5) Backstroke, Freestyle, Butterfly x 100 6) Backstroke 7) Butterfly 8) Backstroke, Freestyle, Butterfly x 100 9) Butterfly
Swim, Kick, Drill	8x100	No Fins, Done As 1) Breaststroke 2) Breaststroke 3) Delayed Breaststroke 4) Breaststroke Kick 5) Breaststroke 6) Breaststroke 7) Delayed Breaststroke 8) Breaststroke Kick
Warm-down	1000 1000	Kick, With Fins Your Choice Swim, With Fins Your Choice

Week Six – Tuesday PM – 10,000 Long		
Warm-up	1000 1000	Kick, With Fins Your Choice Swim, No Fins Your Choice
Main Set	3x500 3x500 2x500 2x500 2x500	Freestyle Swim Freestyle Pull Breaststroke Swim Backstroke Swim Backstroke Pull
Warm-down	1000 1000	Kick, With Fins Your Choice Swim, With Fins Your Choice

Week Six – Tuesday – Weights

Session Two

- Pull Down Front
- Curls
- Elbow Raises
- Two Form Dips
- Back Lifts
- Squats
- 15min. Bike

Week Six – Wednesday AM – 8000 Mixed

Warm-up	1500	Kick, With Fins Your Choice
	1500	Swim, No Fins Your Choice
Swim	20x50	Butterfly, No Fins
Main Set	1x400	Individual Medley
	500	Kick, No Fins, Min.100 Breaststroke
	2x200	Breaststroke
	500	Kick, No Fins, Min.100 Breaststroke
	2x100	Breaststroke
Swim	20x50	Backstroke, No Fins
Warm-down	500	Kick, With Fins Your Choice
	500	Swim, With Fins Your Choice

Week Six – Wednesday PM – 6000 Hills

Warm-up	1000	Kick, With Fins Your Choice
	1000	Swim, No Fins Your Choice
Drills	500	
Main Set	7x25	Freestyle, Hills, Swim
	7x25	Butterfly, Hills, Swim
	7x25	Breaststroke, Hills, Kick
	7x25	Backstroke, Hills, Kick
Warm-down	1000	Kick, With Fins Your Choice
	1000	Swim, With Fins Your Choice

Week Six – Wednesday – Weights

Session Three

- Pull Down Front
- Dips
- Dumb Bell Behind Head
- Machine Pull Together
- Tricep Push Downs
- Leg Raises
- 15min. Bike

Week Six – Thursday AM – 7500 Kick

Warm-up	1500	Swim, No Fins Your Choice	
	1500	Pull, No Fins Your Choice	
Main Set	4x300	Kick, Each 300 Done As	100 Freestyle 100 Backstroke 100 Butterfly
	6x300	Kick, Done As	1) 300 Freestyle 2) 300 Backstroke 3) 300 Butterfly 4) 300 Freestyle 5) 300 Backstroke 6) 300 Butterfly
	500	Kick, No Fins, Min.100 Breaststroke	
Warm-down	1000	Swim, With Fins Your Choice	

Week Six – Thursday PM – 10,000 Long

Warm-up	1000	Kick, With Fins Your Choice
	1000	Swim, No Fins Your Choice
Main Set	2x1500	Swim, Freestyle
	1x1500	Pull, Freestyle
	1x1500	Swim, Backstroke
Warm-down	1000	Kick, With Fins Your Choice
	1000	Swim, With Fins Your Choice

Week Six – Thursday – Weights

Session Four

- Seated Rows
- Bench Press
- Bend Over Rows
- Machine Push Aparts
- Cleans
- Hamstrings
- 15min. Bike

Week Six – Friday AM – 6000 Mixed		
Swim	1000	No Fins Your Choice
Kick	1500	With Fins Your Choice
Pull	1000	No Fins Your Choice
Swim	1000	Individual Medley, With Fins Your Choice Done As 100 Butterfly 200 Individual Medley 100 Backstroke 200 Individual Medley 100 Breaststroke 200 Individual Medley 100 Freestyle
Kick	1500	With Fins Your Choice

Week Six – Friday PM – 8000 Medley		
Set One, No Fins	4x1000	1) Swim, Freestyle, No Fins 2) Swim, Backstroke, No Fins 3) Pull, Freestyle, No Fins 4) Pull, Backstroke, No Fins
Set Two, With Fins	4x700	1) Kick, Freestyle, With Fins 2) Kick, Backstroke, With Fins 3) Kick, Butterfly, With Fins 4) Kick, Freestyle, With Fins
Set Three	4x200	Swim, Individual Medley, No Fins
Set Four	4x100	Swim, Breaststroke, No Fins

Week Six – Friday – Weights

Session One

- Pull Down Behind
- Chin Ups
- Flies
- Wrist Curls
- Forearm Pull Downs
- Sit Ups
- 15min. Bike

Week Six – Saturday AM – 10,000 Waitakeres		
Warm-up	1000 1000	Kick, With Fins Your Choice Swim, No Fins Your Choice
Main Set	4x100 8x100 16x100	Butterfly, With Fins Breaststroke Backstroke, Pull
Kick	1000	Kick, With Fins Your Choice
Main Set	32x100	Freestyle, Pull
Warm-down	1000	Swim, With Fins Your Choice

Week Six – Saturday PM – 5000 Kick			
Warm-up	1000 1000	Kick, With Fins Your Choice Swim, No Fins Your Choice	
Drills	500		
Stroke Correction	800		
Kick	3x400	With Fins,	1) Freestyle 2) Backstroke 3) Butterfly
Kick	500	Breaststroke	

Week Six – Sunday AM – 8000 Mixed		
Warm-up	2000	No Fins Your Choice
Swim	20x50	Butterfly , No Fins
Kick	2000	With Fins Your Choice
Swim	20x50	Backstroke, No Fins
Pull	2000	No Fins Your Choice

Week Six- Sunday – Weights

Session Two

- Pull Down Front
- Curls
- Elbow Raises
- Two Form Dips
- Back Lifts
- Squats
- 15min. Bike

NOTES TO WEEK SIX SCHEDULES

The most significant change to this week's program is the introduction on Wednesday afternoon of "Hills". This session gets its name from the weeks of hill running Lydiard uses to effect the transition from 100 miles a week of conditioning running to trials and coordination speed work on the track. In deference to its Lydiard origins we decided to call the swimming session that eases the same transition by the same name. It is important to have a transition mechanism. Swimmers' muscles have become used to miles of steady swimming. But it will soon be time for the race specific end of the season to begin. A Hills session is not however speed work. It does represent a lifting of the tempo from all that has gone before, but it is certainly not a series of flat-out sprints. The athlete swims 25m in a specified number of strokes, at about 70% effort. For example Jane Copland and Nichola Chellingworth would normally swim 25m in the build-up in 13/14 freestyle strokes. In the Hills 25m this increases to 16/18 strokes. In breaststroke the change is from 5 to 7 strokes. By increasing the rhythm and tempo of these swims, the swimmers can ensure their technique remains sound as they adjust to the speeds that will be expected in the anaerobic and racing periods. As was reported in Swim to the Top, "During one transition period, Nichola Chellingworth swam her first session of 25m Hills in an average time of 13.58s (from a push-off) at a stroke rate of 0.71s. Five weeks later, she swam her last session in an average of 12.47s at a stroke rate of 0.54s. She was ready for the business end of the season to begin."

With the exception of the introduction of Hills, the next five weeks copy the first five weeks. In the case of the Tuesday, Thursday and Saturday long sessions the repetition allows swimmers to evaluate progress by comparing the speed of the same set in the first and second five weeks. It is important that the comparison is genuine. There is no benefit in swimming a good aerobic effort in the first five weeks and then winding up into an anaerobic gut-buster in the second five weeks. Both efforts must be comparable and aerobic for the comparison to have any meaning. If some of the long sets in the second five weeks are not faster, there is no reason for concern. Material progress in aerobic conditioning is more usually seen from season to season rather than within the same season. I recall Genadi Touretski, the exceptional Russian swimming coach, being asked what he thought was the most important quality in good coaching. He said, "Patience." He is right, especially when it comes to aerobic conditioning. Physiological gains may take time, but when they do occur they are deep seated and long lasting.

A drill included in the schedules is the breaststroke drill, Delayed Kick. The drill is done by completing a full breaststroke arm stroke, then waiting three or four seconds before doing the breaststroke kick. It is a new and most important drill. The timing of modern breaststroke is quite different from the breaststroke swum years ago. Today, the later the kick is made in the stroke, the better. The principle is that a late kick allows time for the swimmer to get the arm stroke almost completed and the arms and body streamlined prior to the kick taking place. The kick is far more effective. Time spent on this drill and incorporating its lessons into a swimmer's normal stroke will be time well spent.

By week six of the build-up, the weights lifted will be getting near the maximum possible while still holding 3 x 7 repetitions. Because the weights are really heavy, I allow swimmers to reduce the repetitions to 3 x 6 when the weight of an exercise is first increased. The weight of different exercises will not increase uniformly. Jane and Nichola loved Chin Ups and Elbow Raises. Toni Jeffs was best at Dips and Machine Push Aparts – she was mind blowingly good at Dips. All three were only average at the Bench Press for some reason.

I have seen a number of squads make two serious errors in the management of their weight training program. Some squads replace one or more swimming sessions with weights. This is wrong. Swimming training is still the best form of training for swimming. Weights are an extra to be done over and above a full program of swimming. They are not and must never be a replacement for missed swimming sessions. Other squads do weights for limited periods – in the winter months, during training camps or over school holidays. This is a waste of time and money. Gains in strength from lifting weights occur quickly and so do losses when weights are stopped. Once swimmers start using weights they must be continued if the strength gains are to benefit competitive performances. Weights should continue up to two or three days prior to the season's main event. The amount lifted should be reduced in the last two or three weeks before the season's main event, but if swimmers stop completely they may as well have not started in the first place.

YOUNGER AND LESS EXPERIENCED SWIMMERS

Young swimmers who aim to progress up to 100 kilometers can initially adjust the schedules in this book by cutting back on the number of repetitions or reducing the length of each repetition. In the first week after moving to a Lydiard program, I aim to have young swimmers swim once a day for seven days. In each session I set the same schedule but halve the distance done by swimmers doing the full program – 3x2000m becomes 3x1000m and 1000m warm-up becomes 500m and so on. This normally results in a weekly distance of around 33 kilometers. As the weeks go by I keep the number of sessions at seven, but increase the distance of each session up to 75% of the full program – increasing the weekly distance swum to 45 kilometers. At this point I introduce what the Americans call, "doubles" – that's swimming twice a day. Just one day of doubles to start with then two until the new swimmer is at six days of doubles and one single. By that stage the mileage will be around 80 kilometers and the swimmer will be ready for the final push to 100 kilometers. This process normally takes a good worker around two years to complete.

WEEK SEVEN SCHEDULES

Week Seven – Monday AM – 6000 Mixed				
Warm-up	1000	Kick, With Fins Your Choice		
Swim	5 x 200	Done As		1) Butterfly 2) Backstroke 3) Breaststroke 4) Freestyle 5) Individual Medley
Kick	1000	Kick, With Fins Your Choice		
Swim	10 x 100	Freestyle		
Kick	1000	Done As	200 800	Breaststroke No Fins Your Choice
Swim	20 x 50	Done As	5x50	Each Stroke

Week Seven – Monday PM – 8000 Individual Medley

Set One – No Fins
1000 Backstroke Swim
700 Freestyle Swim
200 Breaststroke Swim
100 Breaststroke Kick

Set Two – With Fins
1000 Butterfly / Butterfly Drills, Your Choice Of Mix
700 Freestyle Kick
200 Backstroke Kick
100 Butterfly Kick

Set Three – No Fins
1000 Backstroke Pull
700 Freestyle Pull
200 Breaststroke Swim
100 Breaststroke Kick

Set Four – With Fins
1000 Individual Medley, Done As 1x400, 1x200, 1x400 Individual Medley
700 Freestyle Kick
200 Backstroke Kick
100 Butterfly Kick

Week Seven – Tuesday AM – 7500 Kick		
Warm-up	1500	Swim, No Fins Your Choice
	1000	Kick, With Fins Your Choice
Swim	5x100	Butterfly
Kick	200	Butterfly, No Fins
	300	Butterfly, With Fins
Swim	5x100	Backstroke
Kick	200	Backstroke, No Fins
	300	Backstroke, With Fins
Swim	5x100	Breaststroke
Kick	500	Breaststroke
Swim	5x100	Freestyle
Kick	200	Freestyle, No Fins
	300	Freestyle, With Fins
Warm-down	1000	Swim, With Fins Your Choice

Week Seven – Tuesday PM – 10,000 Long		
Warm-up	1000	Kick, With Fins Your Choice
	1000	Swim, No Fins Your Choice
Main Set	5x400	Freestyle Swim
	4x400	Freestyle Pull
	2x400	Breaststroke Swim
	2x400	Backstroke Swim
	2x400	Backstroke Pull
Warm-down	1000	Kick, With Fins Your Choice
	1000	Swim, With Fins Your Choice

Week Seven – Tuesday – Weights

Session Three

- Pull Down Front
- Dips
- Dumb Bell Behind Head
- Machine Pull Together
- Tricep Push Downs
- Leg Raises
- 15min. Bike

Week Seven – Wednesday AM – 8000 Mixed

Warm-up	1000	Kick, With Fins Your Choice
	1000	Swim, No Fins Your Choice
	1000	Pull, No Fins Your Choice
Main Set	16x200	Individual Medley
Warm-down	1000	Kick, With Fins Your Choice
	800	Swim, With Fins Your Choice

Week Seven – Wednesday PM – 6000 Hills

Warm-up	1000	Kick, With Fins Your Choice
	1000	Swim, No Fins Your Choice
Drills	500	
Main Set	7x25	Breaststroke, Hills, Swim
	7x25	Backstroke, Hills, Swim
	7x25	Freestyle, Hills, Kick
	7x25	Butterfly, Hills, Kick
Warm-down	1000	Kick, With Fins Your Choice
	1000	Swim, With Fins Your Choice

Week Seven – Wednesday – Weights

Session Four

- Seated Rows
- Bench Press
- Bend Over Rows
- Machine Push Aparts
- Cleans
- Hamstrings
- 15min. Bike

Week Seven – Thursday AM – 7500 Kick

Warm-up	1500	Swim, No Fins Your Choice
	1500	Pull, No Fins Your Choice
Main Set	3000	Kick, With Fins Your Choice
	500	Kick, No Fins, Min.100 Breaststroke
Warm-down	1000	Swim, With Fins Your Choice

Week Seven – Thursday PM – 10,000 Long

Warm-up	1000	Kick, With Fins Your Choice
	1000	Swim, No Fins Your Choice
Main Set	2x1000	Swim, Freestyle
	1x1000	Pull, Freestyle
	1x1000	Swim, Individual Medley
	1x1000	Swim, Backstroke
	1x1000	Pull, Backstroke
Warm-down	1000	Kick, With Fins Your Choice
	1000	Swim, With Fins Your Choice

Week Seven – Thursday – Weights

Session One

- Pull Down Behind
- Chin Ups
- Flies
- Wrist Curls
- Forearm Pull Downs
- Sit Ups
- 15min. Bike

Week Seven – Friday AM – 6000 Mixed			
Swim	1000	No Fins Your Choice	
Kick	1500	With Fins Your Choice	
Pull	1000	No Fins Your Choice	
Swim	1000	Individual Medley, With Fins Your Choice	
		Done As	100 Butterfly
			200 Individual Medley
			100 Backstroke
			200 Individual Medley
			100 Breaststroke
			200 Individual Medley
			100 Freestyle
Kick	1500	With Fins Your Choice	

Week Seven – Friday PM – 6000 Mixed		
Set One	2000	Swim, Freestyle, No Fins
	1200	Kick, Freestyle, With Fins
	800	Pull, Freestyle, No Fins
Set Two	1400	Swim, Backstroke, No Fins
	800	Kick, Backstroke, With Fins
	400	Pull, Backstroke, No Fins
Set Three	800	Swim, Individual Medley, No Fins
	400	Kick, Individual Medley, With Fins Except Breast
	200	Swim, Individual Medley, No Fins

Week Seven – Friday – Weights

Session Two

- Pull Down Front
- Curls
- Elbow Raises
- Two Form Dips
- Back Lifts
- Squats
- 15min. Bike

Week Seven – Saturday AM – 10,000 Waitakeres		
Warm-up	1000	Kick, With Fins Your Choice
Swim / Pull	20x100	Freestyle, Done As 10xSwim, 10xPull
Kick	1000	Kick, With Fins Your Choice
Swim / Pull	20x100	Backstroke, Done As 10xSwim, 10xPull
Kick	1000	Kick, With Fins Your Choice
Swim	20x100	Individual Medley, Swim
Warm-down	1000	Swim, With Fins Your Choice

Week Seven – Saturday PM – 5000 Kick			
Warm-up	1000 1000	Kick, With Fins Your Choice Swim, No Fins Your Choice	
Drills	500		
Stroke Correction	800		
Kick	3x400	With Fins,	1) Freestyle 2) Backstroke 3) Butterfly
Kick	500	Breaststroke	

Week Seven – Sunday AM – 8000 Mixed		
Warm-up	2000	No Fins Your Choice
Swim	20x50	Freestyle, No Fins
Kick	2000	With Fins Your Choice
Swim	20x50	Breaststroke
Pull	2000	No Fins Your Choice

Week Seven – Sunday – Weights

Session Three

- Pull Down Front
- Dips
- Dumb Bell Behind Head
- Machine Pull Together
- Tricep Push Downs
- Leg Raises
- 15min. Bike

NOTES TO WEEK SEVEN SCHEDULES

Applying Lydiard's training principles to the sport of swimming has received more than its fair share of criticism. Bret Naylor, a former New Zealand national coach, told me," In swimming, it will never work." In January 2000 he told Jane Copland she would never be any good because Lydiard's training was, "Wrong for swimming." The National Multi-Disability Coach was reported to have called Lydiard's methods "Old hat." A leading official in a large New Zealand club asked coaches being interviewed for their Head Coach's job, "You don't believe in that Arthur Lydiard stuff, do you?" The only justification Lydiard needs is a bucket full of Olympic medals. However, it is worthwhile spending some time looking at the theory of Lydiard's ideas – just so the doubters know the whole thing is not just a stab in the dark.

The first and most obvious feature is the large amount of time spent developing each physiological characteristic separately; ten weeks on aerobic conditioning, four weeks on anaerobic fitness and ten weeks on race preparation. Few other programs make this stark distinction. They tend to include elements of the different types of training in each month's, or each week's, or even each day's training. Lydiard however is right. The International Center For Aquatic Research (ICAR) has found, "the energy systems (aerobic and anaerobic) adapt independently" and at different rates to "each other to specific modes of training. This is supported by the changes observed in the biochemical markers, PFK and CS. Each of these enzymes changed only in response to specific training: PFK to sprint training, CS to endurance training." Cecil Colwin in his fine book, "Swimming into the 21st Century" said, "The development of improved aerobic capacity is a long, slow process requiring a carefully devised long-term plan; by the same token the resulting adaptations will be retained for a long time." About anaerobic training, however, he says, "When it is done properly, astonishing improvements can be observed in just six weeks. Its effects are short lived and at times appear volatile. The high performance level resulting from this training rarely persist more than three months." The evidence appears to support Lydiard's view that maintaining a clear separation between different types of training is more compatible with the character of each training type and with the way the body adapts than providing several and diverse training stimuli to different energy systems at the same time. In other words, don't mix your training. In the 1950s and 1960s Lydiard may not have known all this scientific stuff, but through practical experience he did know that looking after one thing at a time produced the best result. And that's still true in swimming today.

Lydiard puts this much more simply. He just says runner's and swimmer's hearts and lungs, arteries and veins haven't changed since the 1960s. If keeping different training stimuli separate was the best method of training in the 1960s, why shouldn't it be the best today. Scientists make it sound more technical, but it is the same thing.

The well-known emphasis Lydiard programs put on aerobic conditioning is also widely disputed. This is fundamentally because Lydiard coaches see breaking records and winning championships primarily as endurance, aerobic conditioning problems and not speed. Take the women's 400m world record of just over four minutes. To break it, each 50m must be swum in 30 seconds. In New Zealand alone there are 50 or so women who can do that, each 100m in one minute and there are around 30 who can do that, each 200m in two minutes and there are two or three who can do that. No one, however, can get within ten seconds of four minutes for 400m. Now that is not a speed problem. There are heaps of women with enough basic speed. The problem is they do not have the aerobic conditioning required to maintain their speed for four minutes. Instead of beating New Zealand at 50m freestyle Toni Jeffs, with her basic speed, could have beaten the world at 200m, if she had just been patient enough to establish a well conditioned aerobic base. Susan O'Neil won the women's 200m freestyle at the Sydney Olympic Games. Properly conditioned and swimming 200m, Toni Jeffs could very realistically have expected to beat her. Even the great Ian Thorpe's records are at speeds several New Zealand men and many dozens around the world can swim. There again the problem is aerobic conditioning. The Kenyan and Ethiopian runners beat the world not because of speed, but because they can keep going at speed. The ability to keep going can be trained. The first nation or major group that really takes to this notion in swimming will steal the same march on the swimming world that Lydiard did in athletics in Rome in 1960.

Lydiard coaching does not dismiss the vital importance of anaerobic fitness. Too much time is allocated to training the anaerobic system in the next stages of the swimmer's preparation for that to be even remotely true. All this method of coaching claims is that when a well trained anaerobic system is added to an aerobic system that already allows swimmers to swim at very high speeds without needing to call on anaerobic mechanisms, then the finest swims will result. Aerobic conditioning achieves this by allowing the muscles to fire powerfully and for longer periods using replenishable oxygen supplies before the anaerobic system is required to take the athlete further or faster or both. This is most likely the result of more and / or better quality access of oxygen to the muscle firing process. Cecil Colwin in "Swimming into the 21st Century" goes further and suggests that sound aerobic conditioning may also improve the chemical interaction that takes place in order to fire each muscle contraction to such an extent that less waste lactic acid is produced and peak performance can be maintained for longer.

YOUNGER AND LESS EXPERIENCED SWIMMERS

For young swimmers, Saturday mornings Waitakeres session is a special case. It is a daunting mountain of a session but offers huge rewards for athletes educated in how to swim the session well. When Jane Copland began her swimming career, we shortened the 100x100m session by swimming 50m for each 100m. As time went on and she got fitter she began to do more of the repetitions as 100m until she could swim 1x50m then 1x100m through the set. The 1x100m then became two, then three and so on until, in less than 12 months from beginning training, and at 13 years of age, she could swim 100x100m going every 1.30.

Samantha, 6 years old. The distance swum at this age is not likely to cause a problem. It is speed that can harm. The rigors of a full Lydiard program are for the future.

Week Eight – Monday AM – 6000 Mixed			
Warm-up	1000	Kick, With Fins Your Choice	
Swim	5 x 200	Done As	1) Butterfly 2) Backstroke 3) Breaststroke 4) Freestyle 5) Individual Medley
Kick	1000	Kick, With Fins Your Choice	
Swim	10 x 100	Backstroke	
Kick	1000	Done As	200 Breaststroke 800 No Fins Your Choice
Swim	20 x 50	Done As	5x50 Each Stroke

Week Eight – Monday PM – 8000 Individual Medley

Set One – No Fins
2000 Freestyle Swim

Set Two – With Fins
1000 Butterfly / Butterfly Drills, Your Choice Of Mix
500 Freestyle Kick
300 Backstroke Kick
200 Butterfly Kick

Set Three - No Fins
2000 Backstroke Pull

Set Four - With Fins
1000 Individual Medley, Done As 1x400, 1x200, 1x400 Individual Medley
500 Freestyle Kick
300 Backstroke Kick
200 Butterfly Kick

Week Eight – Tuesday AM – 7500 Kick		
Warm-up	2000	Swim, No Fins Your Choice
Kick	9x300	With Fins, Done As 1) Freestyle 2) Backstroke, Freestyle, Butterfly x 100 3) Freestyle 4) Backstroke 5) Backstroke, Freestyle, Butterfly x 100 6) Backstroke 7) Butterfly 8) Backstroke, Freestyle, Butterfly x 100 9) Butterfly
Swim, Kick, Drill	8x100	No Fins, Done As 1) Breaststroke 2) Breaststroke 3) Delayed Breaststroke 4) Breaststroke Kick 5) Breaststroke 6) Breaststroke 7) Delayed Breaststroke 8) Breaststroke Kick
Warm-down	1000 1000	Kick, With Fins Your Choice Swim, With Fins Your Choice

Week Eight – Tuesday PM – 10,000 Long		
Warm-up	1000 1000	Kick, With Fins Your Choice Swim, No Fins Your Choice
Main Set	10x200 8x200 4x200 4x200 4x200	Freestyle Swim Freestyle Pull Breaststroke Swim Backstroke Swim Backstroke Pull
Warm-down	1000 1000	Kick, With Fins Your Choice Swim, With Fins Your Choice

Week Eight – Tuesday – Weights

Session Four

- Seated Rows
- Bench Press
- Bend Over Rows
- Machine Push Aparts
- Cleans
- Hamstrings
- 15min. Bike

Week Eight – Wednesday AM – 8000 Mixed		
Warm-up	1500	Kick, With Fins Your Choice
	1500	Swim, No Fins Your Choice
Swim	20x50	Butterfly, No Fins
Main Set	2x200	Individual Medley
	500	Kick, No Fins, Min.100 Breaststroke
	4x100	Breaststroke
	500	Kick, No Fins, Min.100 Breaststroke
	4x50	Breaststroke
Swim	20x50	Backstroke, No Fins
Warm-down	500	Kick, With Fins Your Choice
	500	Swim, With Fins Your Choice

Week Eight – Wednesday PM – 6000 Hills		
Warm-up	1000	Kick, With Fins Your Choice
	1000	Swim, No Fins Your Choice
Drills	500	
Main Set	7x25	Freestyle, Hills, Swim
	7x25	Butterfly, Hills, Swim
	7x25	Breaststroke, Hills, Kick
	7x25	Backstroke, Hills, Kick
Warm-down	1000	Kick, With Fins Your Choice
	1000	Swim, With Fins Your Choice

Week Eight – Wednesday – Weights

Session One

- Pull Down Behind
- Chin Ups
- Flies
- Wrist Curls
- Forearm Pull Downs
- Sit Ups
- 15min. Bike

Week Eight – Thursday AM – 7500 Kick

Warm-up	1500	Swim, No Fins Your Choice	
	1500	Pull, No Fins Your Choice	
Main Set	4x300	Kick, Each 300 Done As	100 Freestyle 100 Backstroke 100 Butterfly
	6x300	Kick, Done As	1) 300 Freestyle 2) 300 Backstroke 3) 300 Butterfly 4) 300 Freestyle 5) 300 Backstroke 6) 300 Butterfly
	500	Kick, No Fins, Min.100 Breaststroke	
Warm-down	1000	Swim, With Fins Your Choice	

Week Eight – Thursday PM – 10,000 Long

Warm-up	1000	Kick, With Fins Your Choice
	1000	Swim, No Fins Your Choice
Main Set	1x3000	Swim, Freestyle
	1x3000	Pull, Freestyle
Warm-down	1000	Kick, With Fins Your Choice
	1000	Swim, With Fins Your Choice

Week Eight – Thursday – Weights

Session Two

- Pull Down Front
- Curls
- Elbow Raises
- Two Form Dips
- Back Lifts
- Squats
- 15min. Bike

Week Eight – Friday AM – 6000 Mixed		
Swim	1000	No Fins Your Choice
Kick	1500	With Fins Your Choice
Pull	1000	No Fins Your Choice
Swim	1000	Individual Medley, With Fins Your Choice Done As 100 Butterfly 200 Individual Medley 100 Backstroke 200 Individual Medley 100 Breaststroke 200 Individual Medley 100 Freestyle
Kick	1500	With Fins Your Choice

Week Eight – Friday PM – 8000 Medley		
Set One	4x1000	1) Swim, Freestyle, No Fins 2) Swim, Backstroke, No Fins 3) Pull, Freestyle, No Fins 4) Pull, Backstroke, No Fins
Set Two	4x700	1) Kick, Freestyle, With Fins 2) Kick, Backstroke, With Fins 3) Kick, Butterfly, With Fins 4) Kick, Freestyle, With Fins
Set Three	4x200	Swim, Individual Medley, No Fins
Set Four	4x100	Swim, Breaststroke, No Fins

Week Eight – Friday – Weights

Session Three

- Pull Down Front
- Dips
- Dumb Bell Behind Head
- Machine Pull Together
- Tricep Push Downs
- Leg Raises
- 15min. Bike

Week Eight – Saturday AM – 10,000 Waitakeres

Warm-up	1500 1500	Swim, No Fins Your Choice Kick, With Fins Your Choice
Main Set	20x100	Freestyle, 10xSwim, 10xPull
Swim / Kick	1500 1500	Swim, No Fins Your Choice Kick, With Fins Your Choice
Main Set	20x100	Done As 10xBackstroke (5xSwim, 5xPull) 10xIndividual Medley

Week Eight – Saturday PM – 5000 Kick

Warm-up	1000 1000	Kick, With Fins Your Choice Swim, No Fins Your Choice	
Drills	500		
Stroke Correction	800		
Kick	3x400	With Fins	1) Freestyle 2) Backstroke 3) Butterfly
Kick	500	Breaststroke	

Week Eight – Sunday AM – 8000 Mixed		
Warm-up	2000	No Fins Your Choice
Swim	20x50	Butterfly , No Fins
Kick	2000	With Fins Your Choice
Swim	20x50	Backstroke, No Fins
Pull	2000	No Fins Your Choice

Week Eight – Sunday – Weights

Session Four

- Seated Rows
- Bench Press
- Bend Over Rows
- Machine Push Aparts
- Cleans
- Hamstrings
- 15min. Bike

NOTES TO WEEK EIGHT SCHEDULES

Improved training methods will produce significant advances in swimming speeds over the next few years. In twenty years we will look at the times of Thorpe, de Bruin, Klim and O'Neil and say," They weren't all that fast" – just as we do now with the times of Scholander, Rose, Fraser and even Spitz. However, the sector that offers the greatest potential for progress is women's swimming. In just a few decades women have come from nowhere in swimming and sport in general. They have progressed from not being able to compete at all to being able to swim, but compelled to wear more than actresses do today attending the Oscars. Even modern training books almost always have a special chapter on women's training. Women's participation is not quite normal, a sort of, "This book was written with men in mind. If you want to apply it to women's training it should be modified as follows." And the modifications are always less. What percentage of men's training can women handle? Only the most liberal acknowledge women might be able to handle the same volume of training as men. David Emery in his book, World Sporting Records wrote women off in less than half a page. "There are," he said, "unalterable differences which count against women." They have smaller hearts, less blood, less hemoglobin, more fat, poorer sporting shapes and can not deal with hot weather. "Overall," the book concludes, "females have an inferior capacity for physical performance than males." Little wonder I say. Any female reading that could be excused for fleeing the playing field for life in a sanitarium. And it needn't be this way. Women do have advantages that may rapidly improve their sporting standards, or in swimming, their world records.

Three advantages stand out. Studies have shown women convert fat to energy quicker than men. This means they do not burn up their stores of carbohydrate (glycogen) as quickly as men because their bodies are fueled by fat instead. Secondly there seems to be inescapable evidence that women are more contentious about work than men. In New Zealand, women, especially from all female schools, outscore men in national examinations year after year and by a huge percentage. One only has to coach a squad of males and females for a few weeks to know which group has the best application. Thirdly, anecdotal evidence suggests women put up with hardship better and for longer. Many stories exist of woman living longer in conditions of hardship – shipwrecks, being lost, and the like.

All this boils down to one hypothesis. Women genetically, physically and mentally can work harder than men. The books and chapters on women's training address the wrong problem. It is not a question of what percentage of an average male's training should women do. It is a matter of deciding how much more than males the average woman can or possibly should do, to be working at a level that best maximizes her potential. I suspect the answer is a lot more than even elite women are doing now and also a lot more than we would all think. For example if 100km per week swimming is the right distance for an average male's build-up, what is it for women? My guess is that it is around 125km. In other words I believe women are capable of working 25% harder than the average male. The flip side of that of course is that I also think women have to work 25% harder to develop their potential to the same extent as men. They can and they have to. When they do, you watch their records tumble.

It would be convenient to counter this view by saying, "25% harder for the same result. That's not right or fair." The answer is that the potential to work harder is the female genetic advantage. Fair or not, play to that advantage.

An important adjustment required by the 100km per week build-up program is time. Good swimmers can train build-up schedules at round four kilometers an hour, or 25 hours each week for the 100km. Add to this 30 minutes per session to get to the pool, get changed and get wet, plus another 30 minutes to get out, get dressed and get home and the hours increase to 38 per week. Each of the five weight training sessions involves an hour each and the build-up training commitment totals 43 hours per week. That timetable doesn't provide time for discussions with the coach, medical check-ups, physiotherapy, massage, sports science or, and most importantly, rest. Swimmers training at this level require a minimum of one and a half hours sleep each day in addition to the normal eight or nine hours at night. Training is all about subjecting the body to stress and allowing time for recovery. Miss out on the daily rest and recovery and the benefits of training will not eventuate. The commitment is high. Fitting in school, university or work is difficult. There is enough time, but only just. The activity called social life will have to wait. Whether you want a life like this or not depends entirely on whether you want to be one of the world's best swimmers. If you do, this is about what it takes. The data in the table below attempts to show in tabular form the allocation of hours discussed in these notes. Not all the daily hours multiplied by seven equal the weekly hours. This is because not all daily things are done every day. Swimming training is 13 sessions for example, not 14 and weights are five not seven.

SWIMMER DAILY AND WEEKLY SCHEDULE

ACTIVITY	HOURS PER DAY	HOURS PER WEEK
NIGHT SLEEP	8.0	56.0
DAY SLEEP	1.5	10.5
TRAINING SWIMMING	4.0	25.0
TRAINING WEIGHTS	1.0	5.0
TRAVEL	2.0	13.0
EATING	1.0	7.0
SCHOOL	4.5	31.5
OTHER	2.0	20.0
TOTALS	24.0	168.0

YOUNGER AND LESS EXPERIENCED SWIMMERS

Many triathletes are wonderful swimmers. I have included them in the section on "less experienced swimmers" only because they are not specialist pool swimmers and cannot be expected to swim 100kms each week. If they did, there would never be time to ride their bike or run. The table below shows the weekly training distances recommended for an experienced triathlete through a full training season.

TRIATHLON TRAINING DISTANCES

	PERIOD	WEEKLY DISTANCE – KMS
Build-up	18 Weeks	35
Transition	2 Weeks	30
Trials and Coordination	3 Weeks	20
Trials and Coordination	1 Week	14
Trials and Coordination	1 Week	10
TOTALS	25 Weeks	774

Reducing the pool swimmer's schedules for triathlon training is best done by cutting back in the manner recommended for less experienced swimmers – reducing the number or length of the repetitions while still preserving the physiological intent of the session. For top, experienced triathletes I recommend a weekly program of four sessions. It is important the sessions selected from the competitive swimmer's weekly program preserve the balance of the training. There would be no point in swimming four mixed recovery sessions or four kick sessions. The training would not be balanced. The table below shows the schedules I recommend experienced triathletes should select during the build-up period.

BUILD-UP – RECOMENDED TRIATHLETE SCHEDULE SELECTION

Schedule	Swim Session	Distance	Purpose
Long	Thu PM	10000	Aerobic Conditioning
Mixed	Wed AM	8000	Mixed Recovery
Waitakeres	Sat AM	10000	Aerobic Conditioning
Mixed, Kick	Thu AM	7500	Kick And Recovery
TOTAL	4	35500	

Winning Masters Triathletes – Theresa and Paul enjoy the spoils of victory in a US Virgin Islands Masters competition. Masters swimming, track and cycling events are wonderful additions to the sporting world.

WEEK NINE SCHEDULES

Week Nine – Monday AM – 6000 Mixed			
Warm-up	1000	Kick, With Fins Your Choice	
Swim	5 x 200	Done As	1) Butterfly 2) Backstroke 3) Breaststroke 4) Freestyle 5) Individual Medley
Kick	1000	Kick, With Fins Your Choice	
Swim	10 x 100	Butterfly	
Kick	1000	Done As 200 Breaststroke 800 No Fins Your Choice	
Swim	20 x 50	Done As 5 x 50 Each Stroke	

Week Nine – Monday PM – 8000 Individual Medley

Set One – No Fins
1000 Freestyle Swim
700 Backstroke Swim
200 Breaststroke Swim
100 Breaststroke Kick

Set Two – With Fins
1000 Butterfly / Butterfly Drills, Your Choice Of Mix
700 Freestyle Kick
200 Backstroke Kick
100 Butterfly Kick

Set Three - No Fins
1000 Freestyle Pull
700 Backstroke Pull
200 Breaststroke Swim
100 Breaststroke Kick

Set Four - With Fins
1000 Individual Medley
700 Freestyle Kick
200 Backstroke Kick
100 Butterfly Kick

Week Nine – Tuesday AM – 7500 Kick		
Warm-up	1500	Swim, No Fins Your Choice
	1000	Kick, With Fins Your Choice
Swim	5x100	Butterfly
Kick	200	Butterfly, No Fins
	300	Butterfly, With Fins
Swim	5x100	Backstroke
Kick	200	Backstroke, No Fins
	300	Backstroke, With Fins
Swim	5x100	Breaststroke
Kick	500	Breaststroke
Swim	5x100	Freestyle
Kick	200	Freestyle, No Fins
	300	Freestyle, With Fins
Warm-down	1000	Swim, With Fins Your Choice

Week Nine – Tuesday PM – 10,000 Long		
Warm-up	1000	Kick, With Fins Your Choice
	1000	Swim, No Fins Your Choice
Main Set	3x800	Freestyle Swim
	2x800	Freestyle Pull
	1x400	Individual Medley Swim
	1x800	Backstroke Swim
	1x800	Backstroke Pull
Warm-down	1000	Kick, With Fins Your Choice
	1000	Swim, With Fins Your Choice

Week Nine – Tuesday – Weights

Session One

- Pull Down Behind
- Chin Ups
- Flies
- Wrist Curls
- Forearm Pull Downs
- Sit Ups
- 15min. Bike

Week Nine – Wednesday AM – 8000 Mixed

Warm-up	1000	Kick, With Fins Your Choice
	1000	Swim, No Fins Your Choice
	1000	Pull, No Fins Your Choice
Main Set	8x400	Individual Medley
Warm-down	1000	Kick, With Fins Your Choice
	800	Swim, With Fins Your Choice

Week Nine – Wednesday PM – 6000 Hills

Warm-up	1000	Kick, With Fins Your Choice
	1000	Swim, No Fins Your Choice
Drills	500	
Main Set	7x25	Breaststroke, Hills, Swim
	7x25	Backstroke, Hills, Swim
	7x25	Freestyle, Hills, Kick
	7x25	Butterfly, Hills, Kick
Warm-down	1000	Kick, With Fins Your Choice
	1000	Swim, With Fins Your Choice

Week Nine – Wednesday – Weights	

Session Two

- Pull Down Front
- Curls
- Elbow Raises
- Two Form Dips
- Back Lifts
- Squats
- 15min. Bike
- 15min. Bike

Week Nine – Thursday AM – 7500 Kick		
Warm-up	1500	Swim, No Fins Your Choice
	1500	Pull, No Fins Your Choice
Main Set	3000	Kick, With Fins Your Choice
	500	Kick, No Fins, Min.100 Breaststroke
Warm-down	1000	Swim, With Fins Your Choice

Week Nine – Thursday PM – 10,000 Long		
Warm-up	1000	Kick, With Fins Your Choice
	1000	Swim, No Fins Your Choice
Main Set	1x2000	Swim, Freestyle
	1x2000	Pull, Freestyle
	1x2000	Swim, Backstroke
Warm-down	1000	Kick, With Fins Your Choice
	1000	Swim, With Fins Your Choice

Week Nine – Thursday – Weights

Session Three

- Pull Down Front
- Dips
- Dumb Bell Behind Head
- Machine Pull Together
- Tricep Push Downs
- Leg Raises
- 15min. Bike

Week Nine – Friday AM – 6000 Mixed

Swim	1000	No Fins Your Choice
Kick	1500	With Fins Your Choice
Pull	1000	No Fins Your Choice
Swim	1000	Individual Medley, With Fins Your Choice Done As 100 Butterfly 200 Individual Medley 100 Backstroke 200 Individual Medley 100 Breaststroke 200 Individual Medley 100 Freestyle
Kick	1500	With Fins Your Choice

Week Nine – Friday PM – 8000 Medley

Set One	2000	Swim, Freestyle, No Fins
	1200	Kick, Freestyle, With Fins
	800	Pull, Freestyle, No Fins
Set Two	1400	Swim, Backstroke, No Fins
	800	Kick, Backstroke, With Fins
	400	Pull, Backstroke, No Fins
Set Three	800	Swim, Individual Medley, No Fins
	400	Kick, Individual Medley, With Fins Except Breaststroke
	200	Swim, Individual Medley, No Fins

Week Nine – Friday – Weights

Session Four

- Seated Rows
- Bench Press
- Bend Over Rows
- Machine Push Aparts
- Cleans
- Hamstrings
- 15min. Bike

Week Nine – Saturday AM – 10,000 Waitakeres

Swim	100x100	Freestyle

Week Nine – Saturday PM – 5000 Kick

Warm-up	1000 1000	Kick, With Fins Your Choice Swim, No Fins Your Choice	
Drills	500		
Stroke Correction	800		
Kick	3x400	With Fins,	1) Freestyle 2) Backstroke 3) Butterfly
Kick	500	Breaststroke	

Week Nine – Sunday AM – 8000 Mixed		
Warm-up	2000	No Fins Your Choice
Swim	20x50	Freestyle, No Fins
Kick	2000	With Fins Your Choice
Swim	20x50	Breaststroke
Pull	2000	No Fins Your Choice

Week Nine – Sunday – Weights

Session One

- Pull Down Behind
- Chin Ups
- Flies
- Wrist Curls
- Forearm Pull Downs
- Sit Ups
- 15min. Bike

NOTES TO WEEK NINE SCHEDULES

An important feature of Week Nine is Saturday's second session of 100x100m. Normally these are swum 1% to 2% faster than the same set in Week Ffive. The conditions for an improvement are ideal. The build-up is almost complete. The athlete will be finding the 100km distance more manageable and the influence of Wednesday's Hills session will have had some sharpening effect. There is no need for concern if the session is not as fast. Not every day produces personal bests, especially in aerobic conditioning where the long term is the important thing.

By Week Nine the swimmer should be lifting significantly more weight than in Week One. The table below, reproduced from *Swim to the Top*, shows the increase in the weight lifted by Nichola Chellingworth between Week One and Week Ten of her 1996/97 build-up.

NICHOLA CHELLINGWORTH – WEIGHTS LIFTED

EXERCISE	WEEK 1	WEEK 10
PULL DOWNS	68 KGS	102 KGS
DIPS	0 KGS	11 KGS
CHIN UPS	0 KGS	10 KGS
FLYS	15 KGS	17 KGS
SQUATS	150 KGS	200 KGS
ELBOW RAISES	30 KGS	46 KGS
TRI. PUSH DOWNS	22 KGS	32 KGS

Nichola had just won the New Zealand Open Women's 50m freestyle title when she began this build-up, so she was not starting off as a weight training novice – but she still improved in the ten weeks by the amounts shown.

In every build-up the number of strokes swum to each length is very important. Every length, whatever the stroke, must be swum in a predetermined number of strokes. As the build-up progresses, and certainly from build-up to build-up, the swimmer must make every effort to bring the number of strokes per length down while maintaining or even improving swimming speed. It is beyond belief the number of swimmers and squads who ignore the importance of stroke numbers. I know of a squad where the senior swimmers take 22-24 freestyle strokes per 25m length for everything from the warm-up to one length sprints. They clearly have never been taught the basics of their trade. Coaches that clearly have no knowledge or interest in the number of strokes their swimmers take to swim a length degrade their qualifications. They are tutors in politics unaware of Aristotle, journalists who don't know when to use an apostrophe.

A number of commentators have promoted the benefits of cross training. When I first heard the term, I thought it meant training in a bad mood, "I'm not cross training, I'm bloody furious." I've heard of support for running, basketball, touch rugby, surf lifesaving and even skiing – or was it hang-gliding. Toni Jeffs spent some time trying to convince New Zealand that riding a bike was the best way to swim a length of the pool. It's all a load of nonsense of course. I do get swimmers to do 15 minutes of stationary cycling during their weight sessions, but the best training for swimming is swimming. If you do all the swimming involved in these schedules, and the weights, I would be surprised if you still wanted to run or play touch rugby. If by some chance you do, go for another swim. It'll do you more good.

No mention has been made of dry land stretching in these schedules. This is because I am opposed to the stretching routines undertaken by many squads prior to training or racing. Physiologists and coaches instruct swimmers never to stretch passed the point of hurting and then extol the benefit of achieving the maximum stretch, of being the supplest. Hurt is a relative term, one man's hurt is another's mild discomfort. I am convinced many of the injuries in swimming and other sports begin as small muscle tears caused as athletes strive to maximize their suppleness. Not one of my athletes has ever had a muscle injury. An outcome that I believe is related directly to the absence of dry land stretching. This is not to say I am against flexibility. How it is best achieved is the question. I prefer and rely on the 500m of 20 stroke drills included in these schedules. They are non-violent, very swimming specific, involve all the swimming strokes and provide good flexibility. Certainly no physiological test undertaken by my swimmers has ever found any lack of flexibility. In fact their flexibility scores have been very good. Do the swimming drills in these schedules well and they will provide swimmers with ample flexibility and at a negligible risk of injury.

YOUNGER AND LESS EXPERIENCED SWIMMERS

Master swimmers, surf swimmers and recreational fitness swimmers will probably never have time to do the full build-up program. They can, however, still use these schedules. They should select a balance of schedules that suit the amount of time they have available. Whatever reduction is made, it should preserve the mix of long schedules, mixed recovery schedules, kick schedules, hill schedules and medley schedules, characteristic of the 100km program. Several sample programs for swimmers who can swim between three and six times per week are shown in the table on the next page. No distances are included in the recommended programs. The distance swum will depend on factors such as the swimmer's level of fitness and the time available. Each swimmer should select distances that suit their personal development and circumstances.

WEEKLY PROGRAM MIXES

Three Sessions Per Week	Four Sessions Per Week
1. Mixed Recovery Session 2. Long Session Or Waitakeres 3. Kick Session	1. Long Session 2. Mixed Recovery Session 3. Waitakeres 4. Kick Session
Five Sessions Per Week	**Six Sessions Per Week**
1. Long Session 2. Mixed Recovery Session 3. Hills 4. Waitakeres 5. Kick Session	1. Long Session 2. Mixed Recovery Session 3. Long Session 4. Hills 5. Waitakeres 6. Kick Session

Iain Trousdell – a New Zealand 50m freestyle Champion Masters swimmer discusses training with legendary track coach, Arthur Lydiard.

Week Ten – Monday AM – 7000 Mixed			
Warm-up	1000	Kick, With Fins Your Choice	
Swim	5 x 200	Done As	1) Butterfly 2) Backstroke 3) Breaststroke 4) Freestyle 5) Individual Medley
Kick	1000	Kick, With Fins Your Choice	
Swim	10 x 100	Freestyle	
Kick	1000	Done As 200 800	Breaststroke No Fins Your Choice
Swim	20 x 50	Done As 5 x 50	Each Stroke
Kick	1000	Kick, With Fins Your Choice	

Week Ten – Monday PM – 8000 Individual Medley

Set One – No Fins
2000 Backstroke Swim

Set Two – With Fins
1000 Butterfly / Butterfly Drills, Your Choice Of Mix
500 Freestyle Kick
300 Backstroke Kick
200 Butterfly Kick

Set Three – No Fins
2000 Freestyle Pull

Set Four – With Fins
1000 Individual Medley, Done As 1x400, 1x200, 1x400 Individual Medley
500 Freestyle Kick
300 Backstroke Kick
200 Butterfly Kick

Week Ten – Tuesday AM – 7500 Kick		
Warm-up	2000	Swim, No Fins Your Choice
Kick	9x300	With Fins, Done As 1) Freestyle 2) Backstroke, Freestyle, Butterfly x 100 3) Freestyle 4) Backstroke 5) Backstroke, Freestyle, Butterfly x 100 6) Backstroke 7) Butterfly 8) Backstroke, Freestyle, Butterfly x 100 9) Butterfly
Swim, Kick, Drill	8x100	No Fins, Done As 1) Breaststroke 2) Breaststroke 3) Delayed Breaststroke 4) Breaststroke Kick 5) Breaststroke 6) Breaststroke 7) Delayed Breaststroke 8) Breaststroke Kick
Warm-down	1000 1000	Kick, With Fins Your Choice Swim, With Fins Your Choice

Week Ten – Tuesday PM – 10,000 Long		
Warm-up	1000 1000	Kick, With Fins Your Choice Swim, No Fins Your Choice
Main Set	3x600 2x600 1x600 2x600 2x600	Freestyle Swim Freestyle Pull Individual Medley Swim Backstroke Swim Backstroke Pull
Warm-down	1000 1000	Kick, With Fins Your Choice Swim, With Fins Your Choice

Week Ten – Tuesday – Weights	

Session Two

- Pull Down Front
- Curls
- Elbow Raises
- Two Form Dips
- Back Lifts
- Squats
- 15min. Bike

Week Ten – Wednesday AM – 8000 Mixed		
Warm-up	1500	Kick, With Fins Your Choice
	1500	Swim, No Fins Your Choice
Swim	20x50	Butterfly, No Fins
Main Set	1x400	Individual Medley
	500	Kick, No Fins, Min.100 Breaststroke
	2x200	Breaststroke
	500	Kick, No Fins, Min.100 Breaststroke
	2x100	Breaststroke
Swim	20x50	Backstroke, No Fins
Warm-down	500	Kick, With Fins Your Choice
	500	Swim, With Fins Your Choice

Week Ten – Wednesday PM – 7000 Hills		
Warm-up	1500	Kick, With Fins Your Choice
	1500	Swim, No Fins Your Choice
Drills	500	
Main Set	7x25	Freestyle, Hills, Swim
	7x25	Butterfly, Hills, Swim
	7x25	Breaststroke, Hills, Kick
	7x25	Backstroke, Hills, Kick
Warm-down	1000	Kick, With Fins Your Choice
	1000	Swim, With Fins Your Choice

Week Ten – Wednesday – Weights

Session Three

- Pull Down Front
- Dips
- Dumb Bell Behind Head
- Machine Pull Together
- Tricep Push Downs
- Leg Raises
- 15min. Bike

Week Ten – Thursday AM – 7500 Kick

Warm-up	1500	Swim, No Fins Your Choice	
	1500	Pull, No Fins Your Choice	
Main Set	4x300	Kick, Each 300 Done As	100 Freestyle 100 Backstroke 100 Butterfly
	6x300	Kick, Done As	1) 300 Freestyle 2) 300 Backstroke 3) 300 Butterfly 4) 300 Freestyle 5) 300 Backstroke 6) 300 Butterfly
	500	Kick, No Fins, Min.100 Breaststroke	
Warm-down	1000	Swim, With Fins Your Choice	

Week Ten – Thursday PM – 10,000 Long

Warm-up	1000	Kick, With Fins Your Choice
	1000	Swim, No Fins Your Choice
Main Set	2x1200	Swim, Freestyle
	1x1200	Pull, Freestyle
	1x1200	Swim, Backstroke
	1x1200	Pull, Backstroke
Warm-down	1000	Kick, With Fins Your Choice
	1000	Swim, With Fins Your Choice

Week Ten – Thursday – Weights

Session Four

- Seated Rows
- Bench Press
- Bend Over Rows
- Machine Push Aparts
- Cleans
- Hamstrings
- 15min. Bike

Week Ten – Friday AM – 7000 Mixed

Swim	1500	No Fins Your Choice
Kick	1500	With Fins Your Choice
Pull	1500	No Fins Your Choice
Swim	1000	Individual Medley, With Fins Your Choice Done As 100 Butterfly 200 Individual Medley 100 Backstroke 200 Individual Medley 100 Breaststroke 200 Individual Medley 100 Freestyle
Kick	1500	With Fins Your Choice

Week Ten – Friday PM – 8000 Medley

Set One	4x1000	1) Swim, Freestyle, No Fins 2) Swim, Backstroke, No Fins 3) Pull, Freestyle, No Fins 4) Pull, Backstroke, No Fins
Set Two	4x700	1) Kick, Freestyle, With Fins 2) Kick, Backstroke, With Fins 3) Kick, Butterfly, With Fins 4) Kick, Freestyle, With Fins
Set Three	4x200	Swim, Individual Medley, No Fins
Set Four	4x100	Swim, Breaststroke

Week Ten – Friday – Weights

Session One

- Pull Down Behind
- Chin Ups
- Flies
- Wrist Curls
- Forearm Pull Downs
- Sit Ups
- 15min. Bike

Week Ten – Saturday AM – 6000 Changing

Warm-up	1500 1500	Kick, With Fins Your Choice Swim, No Fins Your Choice
Drills	500	
Main Set	600	Individual Medley Or Breaststroke
Warm-down	1000 1000	Kick, With Fins Your Choice Swim, With Fins Your Choice

Week Ten – Saturday PM – 6000 Kick

Warm-up	1500 1500	Kick, With Fins Your Choice Swim, No Fins Your Choice	
Drills	500		
Stroke Correction	800		
Kick	3x400	With Fins	1) Freestyle 2) Backstroke 3) Butterfly
Kick	500	Breaststroke	

Week Ten – Sunday AM – 8000 Mixed		
Warm-up	2000	No Fins Your Choice
Swim	20x50	Butterfly , No Fins
Kick	2000	With Fins Your Choice
Swim	20x50	Backstroke, No Fins
Pull	2000	No Fins Your Choice

Week Ten – Sunday – Weights

Session Two

- Pull Down Front
- Curls
- Elbow Raises
- Two Form Dips
- Back Lifts
- Squats
- 15min. Bike

NOTES TO WEEK TEN SCHEDULES

The mileage for this week is 96km. The reduction of four kilometers is the result of a change in Saturday morning's training. The ten kilometers Waitakeres schedule is dropped and replaced with the season's first anaerobic session. This schedule owes its origin to a track session used by Arch Jelley, coach of New Zealand's great miler, John Walker. At the same stage of training, Jelley gave Walker an eight lapper, or 3200m time trial. The session stood out so clearly in their minds that several years later when Walker was on the TV program, "This Is Your Life" and was having to guess who the next guest was, Jelley introduced himself with the words," I think, today we'll do an eight lapper." Walker guessed who it was! The length of the trial should vary depending on the swimmer's main event.

"EIGHT LAPPER" TRIAL LENGTHS

SWIMMER'S MAIN EVENT	RECOMENDED LENGTH OF TRIAL
50 (All Strokes)	300
100 and 200 (All Strokes)	600
400 (Free and Individual Medley)	1000
800 (Free, Women Only)	1800
1500 (Free, Men Only)	3000

The recommended distances of the trial mean swimmers who specialize in strokes other than freestyle will normally swim the 600m trial. Non-freestyle specialists should swim the trial in their specialist stroke. The exception is butterfly. Swimming this stroke badly, which over a long distance is easy to do, is worse than not swimming it at all. Butterfly should only be used when the distance can be swum competently and well using butterfly. If it can not, the trial should be swum freestyle. Jane Copland has swum her trials as 600m breaststroke. The times and annual improvement in her trials for her first six training seasons are shown in the table below.

JANE COPLAND – "EIGHT LAPPER" TIMES

SEASON	TIME	% IMPROVEMENT
1	9.18.48	—
2	8.48.01	5.46
3	8.34.35	2.59
4	8.23.70	2.07
5	8.18.01	1.13
6	8.01.50	3.32

The data for Jane Copland is shown, not because the times are the final word in breaststroke swimming, but to demonstrate the amount of improvement that is possible through the long term development of the aerobic energy system. It is important to recall that these improvements in Jane Copland's breaststroke were achieved at a stage of the season before anaerobic or speed training had even begun. Her 200m splits in the season six trial were 2.38.48, 2.43.74, 2.39.28. Given that many female breaststroke swimmers would love to swim 2.38 for 200m breaststroke on its own, let alone at the start of a 600m trial, the data hardly supports the critics who claim a Lydiard swimming program wrecks a swimmer's speed.

The trial must not be swum as a flat out race. Keep in mind that this is still the end of the build-up and swim the trial accordingly. It is a firm controlled effort to be swum strongly, not raced. One way I do this is to reduce the number of strokes swimmers can use. For example, Jane Copland swam the year six trial in eight breaststroke strokes per length when her racing pace required nine strokes. Limiting the stroke count controls the swimmer's tendency to go too fast too soon.

At the end of Week Ten the build-up is complete. The swimmer will be able to look back on ten weeks and 996km of very sound aerobic conditioning. Jane Copland once did an extra four kilometers on the last Sunday to claim the 1000km in ten weeks badge. In her last six build-ups she has averaged 96km per week. Nichola Chellingworth's best six build-ups averaged 74km and Toni Jeffs best six averaged 80km. All three women were or are national open champions and record holders. Remember, the effect of build-ups is cumulative. Real performance gains accrue only when the swimmer has banked six or seven build-ups. So don't complete a build-up and expect a physical road-to-Damascus experience. A swimmer's performance will benefit a little from the build-up just completed but it is in their cumulative effect that the real profit lies.

An athlete preparing for a major event, such as the World Championships or Olympic Games, should resist the temptation to swim a huge build-up. I've seen it done several times. In their enthusiasm to do well, coach and swimmer devote themselves to swimming large mileages, well beyond anything they have done before. At the Games, the swimmer performs badly and can't understand why. The reason of course is that the most amazing build-up ever will have left the swimmer run-down and tired and will have had no positive effect on the competitive result. Toni Jeffs' poor swim at the Barcelona Olympic Games was because I made this error in her training. I added to it by then setting her speed training that was also too far and too fast. All in all, she didn't have much of a chance. The lesson is that the build-up immediately prior to a major Games should be no more than and preferably less than normal.

It is now time to move on to the next training stages, the transition week followed by the four weeks of anaerobic conditioning.

YOUNGER AND LESS EXPERIENCED SWIMMERS

By Week Ten you will have a good idea of which newly promoted young swimmers are going to survive a Lydiard type conditioning program. Which swimmers justified their promotion and which ones should have been left in the junior squads? Your ratio of success will be best if your selections were made for the right reasons. Certain to fail criteria include: being the son of the Club President, being the daughter of the Club's most ambitious mother, being the son of the Club's nicest or best looking mother. A Lydiard program is no place for imposters or the unprepared. You will be doing no one any favors by promoting swimmers on the basis of privilege or position. Strangely, speed is not always the best standard either. I have often left the fastest swimmer in a junior squad as not yet ready for a Lydiard program. What you are looking for is disciplined application – an ability to work. Promote young swimmers using that measure and your success ratio will be good. When you find a fast one who can also work, you have the best of both worlds – but hard work comes first.

CHAPTER TWO
THE TRANSITION SCHEDULES

On Wednesday afternoon through the last five weeks of the build-up, the session of Hills began the process of preparing the athlete for the race specific training about to begin. The transition week continues this process. As far as possible, it is important not to spring training changes on a swimmer. Allowing a transition period helps avoid injury and prepares the athlete mentally and physically for the testing training ahead. The table below shows the distance of each training session, the daily total distance and the position of each weight training program.

TRANSITION – WEEKLY PROGRAM

DAY	AM/PM	PER SESSION DISTANCE-KM	PER DAY DISTANCE-KM	WEIGHT SESSIONS
MONDAY	AM	6.0		
	PM	6.0	12.0	–
TUESDAY	AM	7.5		
	PM	8.0	15.5	Weights
WED.	AM	6.0		
	PM	6.0	12.0	Weights
THUR.	AM	7.5		
	PM	6.0	13.5	Weights
FRIDAY	AM	6.0		
	PM	8.0	14.0	Weights
SATURDAY	AM	6.0		
	PM	5.0	11.0	–
SUNDAY	AM	7.0		
	PM	–	7.0	Weights
TOTALS		85	85	5

WEEK ELEVEN SCHEDULES

Week Eleven – Monday AM – 6000 Mixed			
Warm-up	1000	Kick, With Fins Your Choice	
Main Set	5x200	Done As	1) Butterfly 2) Backstroke 3) Breaststroke 4) Freestyle 5) Individual Medley
Kick	1000	Kick With Fins Your Choice	
Swim	10x100	Individual Medley Swim 6 – 13 – 6 – 13	
Kick	1000	Done As	200 Breaststroke 800 No Fins Your Choice
Swim	20x50	Swim Done As 5x50 Each Stroke Emphasize Size And Technique Not Speed	

Week Eleven – Monday PM – 6000 Fartlek		
Warm-up	1000 1000	Kick, With Fins Your Choice Swim, No Fins Your Choice
Drills	500	
Main Set	1x1500 1x1000	Fartlek Swim Freestyle Fartlek Kick Individual Medley
Warm-down	500 500	Kick, With Fins Your Choice Swim, With Fins Your Choice

Week Eleven – Tuesday AM – 7500 Kick		
Warm-up	1500	Swim, No Fins Your Choice
	1000	Kick, With Fins Your Choice
Swim	5x100	Butterfly
Kick	200	Butterfly, No Fins
	300	Butterfly, With Fins
Swim	5x100	Backstroke
Kick	200	Backstroke, No Fins
	300	Backstroke, With Fins
Swim	5x100	Breaststroke
Kick	200	Breaststroke, No Fins
	300	Breaststroke, With Fins
Swim	5x100	Freestyle
Kick	200	Freestyle, No Fins
	300	Freestyle, With Fins
Warm-down	1000	Swim, With Fins Your Choice

Week Eleven – Tuesday PM – 8000 Long		
Warm-up	1000	Swim, No Fins Your Choice
	1000	Kick, With Fins Your Choice
Main Set	4x1000	1) Freestyle
		2) Backstroke
		3) Butterfly
		4) Breaststroke
Warm-down	1000	Swim, With Fins Your Choice
	1000	Kick, With Fins Your Choice

Week Eleven – Tuesday – Weights

Session Three

- Pull Down Front
- Dips
- Dumb Bell Behind Head
- Machine Pull Together
- Tricep Push Downs
- Leg Raises
- 15min. Bike

Week Eleven – Wednesday AM – 6000 Mixed

Set One, No Fins	1000	Freestyle, Swim
	700	Backstroke, Swim
	200	Breaststroke, Swim
	100	Breaststroke, Kick
Set Two, No Fins	20x50	5xEach Stroke For Technique Emphasize Size
Set Three, With Fins	1000	Individual Medley
	700	Freestyle, Kick
	200	Backstroke, Kick
	100	Butterfly, Kick
Set Four, No Fins	20x50	5xEach Stroke For Technique Emphasize Size

Week Eleven – Wednesday PM – 6000 Fartlek

Warm-up	1000	Kick, With Fins Your Choice
	1000	Swim, No Fins Your Choice
Drills	500	
Main Set	1x1500	Fartlek, Backstroke Swim
	1x1000	Fartlek, Individual Medley Kick
Warm-down	500	Kick, With Fins Your Choice
	500	Swim, With Fins Your Choice

Week Eleven – Wednesday – Weights

Session Four

- Seated Rows
- Bench Press
- Bend Over Rows
- Machine Push Aparts
- Cleans
- Hamstrings
- 15min. Bike

Week Eleven – Thursday AM – 7500 Mixed

Warm-up	1500	Kick, With Fins Your Choice
	1500	Swim, With Fins Your Choice
Main Set	3000	Kick, With Fins Your Choice
	500	Kick, Breaststroke
Warm-down	1000	Swim, No Fins Your Choice

Week Eleven – Thursday PM – 6000 Hills

Warm-up	1000	Kick, With Fins Your Choice
	1000	Swim, No Fins Your Choice
Drills	500	
Main Set	7x15	Freestyle, Swim Hills
	7x15	Butterfly, Swim Hills
	7x15	Breaststroke, Kick Hills
	7x15	Backstroke, Kick Hills
Warm-down	1000	Kick, With Fins Your Choice
	1000	Swim, With Fins Your Choice

Week Eleven – Thursday – Weights

Session One

- Pull Down Behind
- Chin Ups
- Flies
- Wrist Curls
- Forearm Pull Downs
- Sit Ups
- 15min. Bike

Week Eleven – Friday AM – 6000 Mixed

Warm-up	1000	Kick, With Fins Your Choice
	1000	Swim No Fins Your Choice
Swim	20x50	Done As 5x Each Stroke
Kick	400	Individual Medley
Swim	20x100	Done As 5x Each Stroke
Kick	400	Individual Medley
	200	Breaststroke

Week Eleven – Friday PM – 8000 Mixed

Warm-up	1000	Swim No Fins Your Choice
	1000	Kick With Fins Your Choice
Main Set	8x500	1) Freestyle x2 2) Backstroke x2 3) Butterfly x2 With Fins 4) Breaststroke x2
Warm-down	1000	Swim, With Fins Your Choice
	1000	Kick, With Fins Your Choice

Week Eleven – Friday – Weights

Session Two

- Pull Down Front
- Curls
- Elbow Raises
- Two Form Dips
- Back Lifts
- Squats
- 15min. Bike

Week Eleven – Saturday AM – 6000 Fartlek

Warm-up	1000	Kick, With Fins Your Choice
	1000	Swim, No Fins Your Choice
Drills	500	
Main Set	1x1500	Fartlek
		Done As 750 Butterfly-Easy 25=Freestyle
	750	Breaststroke
		1x1000 Fartlek, Kick Individual Medley
Warm-down	500	Kick, With Fins Your Choice
	500	Swim, With Fins Your Choice

Week Eleven – Saturday PM – 5000 Stroke Correction

Warm-up	1000	Kick, With Fins Your Choice	
	1000	Swim, No Fins Your Choice	
Drills	500		
Main Set	400	Stroke Correction	
Kick	4x400	With Fins, Done As	1) Freestyle
			2) Backstroke
			3) Butterfly
Kick	500	Breaststroke	

Week Eleven – Sunday AM – 7000 Mixed		
Swim	2000	No Fins Your Choice
Kick	1000	With Fins Your Choice
Pull	2000	No Fins Your Choice
Swim	20x50	Freestyle, No Fins
Swim	20x50	Breaststroke

Week Eleven – Sunday – Weights

Session Three

- Pull Down Front
- Dips
- Dumb Bell Behind Head
- Machine Pull Together
- Tricep Push Downs
- Leg Raises
- 15min. Bike

NOTES TO WEEK ELEVEN SCHEDULES

The mileage in the transition week drops to 85km. As the training speeds up, the mileage must come down. Lydiard said, "It's impossible to run a four minute mile and run around the Waitakeres at the same time." At 85km, however, the distance swum in our program is still well above that of many squads in the peak of their distance training. For a swimmer who has just completed ten weeks of 100km, however, the drop to 85km has a marked freshening effect – a further clear signal of the deep reserves of fitness enjoyed by Lydiard conditioned athletes.

The idea that as the athlete's training speeds up, the distance swum should reduce, sounds so logical that the casual reader probably thinks,"Yes, that sounds right. What next?" However, in swimming the idea is not widely accepted at all. In fact most squads try to increase the distance they swim and the speed they swim it at, especially as they get close to a major competition. I know of many local squads who go away to training camps three or four weeks before a championship meet. Some apparently highly qualified coach then attempts to get his charges to swim further than they do at any other time of the year and at a faster speed. National New Zealand training camps used to be notorious for the same reason. It is amazing how something so illogical should be so widely practiced. Mind you, many people used to think the earth was flat.

Four of the transition week's 13 sessions are sharpening swims. On Monday, Wednesday and Saturday a session of fartlek swimming is programmed. Fartlek is a Finnish word meaning speed play and describes a method of running training where the pace is constantly varied. In the pool, fartlek usually involves swimming one length, 25m, fast followed by one length easy through the distance programmed. All transition week fartlek swims are 1500m. The fast segment can be altered to 50m with a recovery of either 25m or 50m. Each of the three sessions also includes 1000m of fartlek kick.

Fartlek has a remarkable sharpening effect – far better than the 15m or 25m sprints used by many squads. Because it is continuous, fartlek replicates the speed of racing without incurring the stress of actual competition. I time each of the fast 25m. The table below shows the improvement in Jane Copland's times for the fartlek 25m over three recent summer seasons. This table is included, not because the times are outstandingly fast, but because they show again the nonsense of the view that build-up conditioning damages an athlete's speed. The butterfly and breaststroke times include the turn at the beginning of the fast length. The backstroke and freestyle times include the turn at the end of each fast length.

JANE COPLAND – FARTLEK TIMES

STROKE	SEASON 2001	SEASON 2000	SEASON 1999
FREE	14.44	15.82	16.80
BREAST	17.86	18.69	18.57
BACK	15.64	17.26	17.70
FLY	15.36	17.26	——

Lydiard does not approve of my timing the fartlek sessions. He is right; the spirit of "speed-play" is pretty much broken when it is done under the watchful eye of a stopwatch. Ideally I would recommend leaving the stopwatch out of these sessions.

The fourth sharpening session is a session of Hills programmed for Thursday afternoon. This is a continuation of the once-a-week Hills sessions included in the last five weeks of the build-up.

Saturday afternoon's stroke correction session continues into the transition week.

The nature of this session, however, should change. During the build-up, stroke correction training can address major stroke changes and make them at modest swimming speeds. By the transition week, however, no more major changes should be made. Coaches and swimmers should now perfect the strokes they have developed and make sure the strokes stay sound at racing speeds. There is a big difference between swimming well slowly and holding the same technique at race pace. At many swim meets, I have noticed that the first thing to suffer when swimmers go fast or get tired is their technique. The stroke correction session should now address the question of technique at speed.

Apart from the four pace and one stroke correction training sessions, the balance of the transition week's training is aerobic conditioning swimming. This serves to consolidate the aerobic gains made during the build-up and provides time for recovery from the new stress of the fartlek swimming.

The introduction of transition training also changes the nature of the program's weight training. Until now every effort has gone into increasing the weights lifted. This must now stop. For each exercise, whatever weight has been achieved by the end of the build-up is the maximum for the season. From now on the aim is to lift the same weight more comfortably, smoother and with better technique. Some squads look on weight training as a means of developing explosive power. I do not agree. Look at the swimming of Popov, de Bruin and Van den Hodenband. All three represent the ultimate in the smooth application of power. Not a grunting explosion in sight. Consolidating the weight lifted and working to achieve easier and smoother lifts through the balance of the season's training is compatible with the objectives being worked on in the pool.

YOUNGER AND LESS EXPERIENCED SWIMMERS

Triathletes swimming 35km in the build-up weeks should swim 30km in the transition week. There is not the same requirement to drop substantially the transition mileage in triathlon training as there is in pool swimming, because the need to go fast is not anything like as great. Remember triathlon swim racing should be an aerobic threshold activity. The lack of anaerobic stress means the weekly training distances can be maintained for longer. The triathlon athlete should do two weeks of transition training by repeating the pool swimmer's one-week program. Two weeks are recommended because the triathlon transition is from build-up to trials and coordination, whereas the pool swimmer is making the less severe change from build-up to anaerobic conditioning.

The table below shows the schedules I recommend triathletes should select during their two transition weeks.

TRANSITION – RECOMENDED TRIATHLETE SCHEDULE SELECTION

Schedule	Distance	Purpose
Long	8000	Aerobic conditioning
Mixed	7000	Mixed recovery
Fartlek	7000	Pace variation
Mixed	8000	Mixed recovery
TOTAL	30000	

CHAPTER THREE
THE ANAEROBIC SCHEDULES

At last the swimmer can begin specific training for the new season's competitions. By now he or she will be chomping at the bit. After ten weeks of steady aerobic pace swimming, the swimmer will want to break out of the speed jail. Over and over again I've heard swimmers say," I can't wait to go fast. I'm going to really go for it now." But they must not. In *Swim to the Top*, the chapter on anaerobic training was called "Anaerobic Training – Festina Lenta". The Latin roughly translated means "make haste slowly". As far as the four weeks anaerobic swimming is concerned, no advice could be more important. When I first discussed the principles of this stage of training with Arthur Lydiard, he used expressions such as," Hold back, keep the tiger in its cage and keep a lid on it." But more than any other he said," It takes very little to sharpen a fit body." And that's the key point. That's why only four weeks are allocated to this first stage of race preparation training. If you do go too hard it can bring your season to a premature end. The swimmer becomes run-down, tired and even quite ill. It's called,"Going over the top." As I said before, it's what happened to Toni Jeffs in Barcelona and it's always serious. When it happens the only cure is to rest.

Danger signs of too much speed training stress include:

1. Frequent mild colds and sore throats
2. Swelling and aching of the lymph glands, in the neck, underarm and groin
3. Skin eruptions among non-adolescents
4. Excessive nervousness, depression, irritability and headaches
5. Nagging fatigue accompanied by an inability to relax or sleep
6. Aching stomach often accompanied by a loss of appetite and weight
7. Diarrhea or constipation
8. Unexplained drops in performance levels
9. Disinterest in normally exciting activities

These signs require corrective action. This means lowering the training stress level by having a week of gentle swimming or even a full week off while the swimmer recovers. The problem is that many coaches prescribe hard work when things are going well and even harder work when they are going badly. I recall one coach who trained a very good backstroke swimmer. At one regional championship I noticed she just wasn't swimming well. Her skin was in terrible condition and I heard she had been affected by several bad colds. The problem was overtraining, the cure was rest. At training the following week I was not surprised to see the swimmer working through a set of 60x25m hard sprints. Her coach clearly had no idea of the damage he was doing. All he understood was she swam slowly, she must need more training. The swimmer lasted a few more months and retired from swimming. If you observe symptoms of overtraining and do nothing, or increase training, the problem will get increasingly severe. Eventually the athlete will need a very long break to recover or, as is often the case, will give the whole sport up as a waste of time.

Anaerobic means, without oxygen. In this instance it is a description of how the energy compound ATP is supplied to the muscle. When the swimmer is swimming sufficiently fast that the oxygen taken in is not enough to continue the supply of ATP, the **balance** of the energy requirement is derived from anaerobic metabolism. Therein lies the key benefit of a Lydiard program. When the efficiency of the aerobic system is lifted so that an increased amount of the energy is supplied aerobically, the balance to be provided anaerobically is less. This is good for the swimmer because anaerobic metabolism has serious disadvantages as an energy source compared to aerobically sourced energy. Firstly it is a less efficient method of producing ATP. The yield of two molecules per molecule of glucose utilized is low. Secondly, the waste product of the break down of glucose is lactic acid. Accumulating lactic acid and oxygen debt become limiting factors to performance and are the source of the discomfort associated with fatigue.

Whereas the previous ten weeks have aimed at reducing the yield of lactate, anaerobic conditioning deliberately sets out to produce a high accumulation of lactic acid, by having the swimmer work at a greatly increased level of intensity. The objective is to improve the swimmer's ability to buffer the accumulation of lactic acid while at the same time limiting to some extent a decrease in pH.

Mileage in the four anaerobic weeks drops again to 80km. The table below shows the distance of each training session, the daily total distance and the position of each weight training program. Even at 80km, the distance swum is still ample to maintain the swimmer's aerobic conditioning.

DAY	AM/PM	PER SESSION DISTANCE-KM	PER DAY DISTANCE-KM	WEIGHT SESSIONS
MONDAY	AM	6.0		
	PM	6.0	12.0	–
TUESDAY	AM	6.0		
	PM	7.0	13.0	Weights
WED.	AM	6.0		
	PM	6.0	12.0	Weights
THUR.	AM	7.0		
	PM	6.0	13.0	Weights
FRIDAY	AM	6.0		
	PM	7.0	13.0	Weights
SATURDAY	AM	6.0		
	PM	5.0	11.0	–
SUNDAY	AM	6.0		
	PM	–	6.0	Weights
TOTALS		80	80	5

WEEK TWELVE SCHEDULES

Week Twelve – Monday AM – 6000 Mixed		
Warm-up	1000	Kick, With Fins Your Choice
	1000	Swim, No Fins Your Choice
Main Set	3000	Swim, No Fins Your Choice
Warm-down	500	Kick, With Fins Your Choice
	500	Swim, With Fins Your Choice

Week Twelve – Monday PM – 6000 Anaerobic		
Warm-up	1000	Kick, With Fins Your Choice
	1000	Swim, No Fins Your Choice
Drills	500	
Swim Throughs	100	
Main Set	6x400	Done As 2x400 Freestyle
		1x400 Breaststroke
		1x400 Backstroke
		1x400 Individual Medley Swim
		1x400 Individual Medley Kick
Warm-down	500	Kick, With Fins Your Choice
	500	Swim, With Fins Your Choice

Week Twelve – Tuesday AM – 6000 Kick			
Warm-up	1000	Swim, No Fins Your Choice	
Main Set	4x300	Kick, With Fins, Done As	1x100 Freestyle 1x100 Backstroke 1x100 Butterfly
	6x300	Kick, With Fins, Done As	2x300 Freestyle 2x300 Backstroke 2x300 Butterfly
	1000	Kick, No Fins, Done As	Individual Medley
Warm-down	1000	Swim, No Fins Your Choice	

Week Twelve – Tuesday PM – 7000 Long			
Warm-up	1000	Kick, With Fins Your Choice	
	1000	Swim, No Fins Your Choice	
Main Set	4x1000	Done As	1) Butterfly 2) Backstroke 3) Breaststroke 4) Freestyle
Warm-down	500	Kick, With Fins Your Choice	
	500	Swim, With Fins Your Choice	

Week Twelve – Tuesday – Weights

Session Four

- Seated Rows
- Bench Press
- Bend Over Rows
- Machine Push Aparts
- Cleans
- Hamstrings
- 15min. Bike

Week Twelve – Wednesday AM – 6000 Individual Medley		
Set One, No Fins	1000	Freestyle, Swim
	700	Backstroke, Swim
	200	Breaststroke, Swim
	100	Breaststroke, Kick
Set Two, With Fins	700	Freestyle, Kick
	200	Backstroke, Kick
	100	Butterfly, Kick
Set Three, No Fins	700	Backstroke, Pull
	200	Breaststroke, Swim
	100	Breaststroke, Kick
Set Four, With Fins	1000	Individual Medley
	700	Freestyle, Kick
	200	Backstroke, Kick
	100	Butterfly, Kick

Week Twelve – Wednesday PM – 6000 Anaerobic		
Warm-up	1000	Kick, With Fins Your Choice
	1000	Swim, No Fins Your Choice
Drills	500	
Swim Throughs	100	
Main Set	45x50	Done As 10x50 Freestyle
		10x50 Breaststroke
		10x50 Backstroke
		3x50 Butterfly
		3x50 Freestyle Kick
		3x50 Breaststroke Kick
		3x50 Backstroke Kick
		3x50 Butterfly Kick
Warm-down	500	Kick, With Fins Your Choice
	500	Swim, With Fins Your Choice

Week Twelve – Wednesday – Weights

Session One

- Pull Down Behind
- Chin Ups
- Flies
- Wrist Curl
- Forearm Pull Downs
- Sit Ups
- 15min. Bike

Week Twelve – Thursday AM – 7000 Kick

Warm-up	1400	Kick, With Fins Your Choice	
Main Set	5x200	Swim, No Fins, Done As	1x Butterfly, With Fins 1x Backstroke 1x Breaststroke 1x Freestyle 1x Individual Medley
	1000	Kick, With Fins Your Choice	
	200	Kick, Breaststroke No Fins	
	100	Kick, Butterfly No Fins	
	10x100	Swim, No Fins, Freestyle	
	1000	Kick, With Fins Your Choice	
	200	Kick, Freestyle No Fins	
	100	Kick, Backstroke No Fins	
	20x50	Swim, No Fins, 5xEach Stroke	

Week Twelve – Thursday PM – 6000 Hills

Warm-up	1000	Kick, With Fins Your Choice
	1000	Swim, No Fins Your Choice
Drills	500	
Main Set	7x15	Freestyle, Swim Hills
	7x15	Butterfly, Swim Hills
	7x15	Breaststroke, Kick Hills
	7x15	Backstroke, Kick Hills
Warm-down	1000	Kick, With Fins Your Choice
	1000	Swim, With Fins Your Choice

Week Twelve – Thursday – Weights

Session Two

- Pull Down Front
- Curls
- Elbow Raises
- Two Form Dips
- Back Lifts
- Squats
- 15min. Bike

Week Twelve – Friday AM – 6000 Mixed

Warm-up	1000	Kick, With Fins Your Choice	
	1000	Swim, No Fins Your Choice	
Main Set	5x200	Swim	5x Individual Medley
			5x Breaststroke
	1000	Kick, Done As	800 With Fins Your Choice
			200 Breaststroke Kick
	10x100	Swim	5x Individual Medley
			5x Breaststroke
Warm-down	500	Kick, With Fins Your Choice	
	500	Swim, With Fins Your Choice	

Week Twelve – Friday PM – 7000 Mixed

Warm-up	1000	Kick, With Fins Your Choice		
	1000	Swim, No Fins Your Choice		
Drills	200	Freestyle Only		
Main Set	7x400	Done As	1) 400	Individual Medley (IM)
			2) 100	IM/50Fly/50Back
			100	IM/50Breast/50Fr
			3) 400	Freestyle Pull
			4) 100	IM/50Fly/50Back
			100	IM/50Breast/50Fr
			5) 400	Individual Medley
			6) 100	IM/50Fly/50Back
			100	IM/50Breast/50Fr
			7) 400	Freestyle Pull
Warm-down	1000	Kick With Fins Your Choice		
	1000	Swim With Fins Your Choice		

Week Twelve – Friday – Weights

Session Three

- Pull Down Front
- Dips
- Dumb Bell Behind Head
- Machine Pull Together
- Tricep Push Downs
- Leg Raises
- 15min. Bike

Week Twelve – Saturday AM – 6000 Anaerobic

Warm-up	1000	Kick, With Fins Your Choice	
	1000	Swim, No Fins Your Choice	
Drills	500		
Swim Throughs	100		
Main Set	16x150	Done As	4x150 Freestyle
			4x150 Breaststroke
			3x150 Backstroke
			1x150 Butterfly
			1x150 Freestyle Kick
			1x150 Breaststroke Kick
			1x150 Backstroke Kick
			1x150 Butterfly Kick
Warm-down	500	Kick, With Fins Your Choice	
	500	Swim, With Fins Your Choice	

Week Twelve – Saturday PM – 5000 Stroke Correction

Warm-up	1000	Kick, With Fins Your Choice	
	1000	Swim, No Fins Your Choice	
Drills	500		
Main Set	800	Stroke Correction	
Kick	3x400	With Fins, Done As	1) Freestyle
			2) Backstroke
			3) Butterfly
Kick	500	Breaststroke	

Week Twelve – Sunday AM – 6000 Mixed		
Swim	2000	No Fins Your Choice
Kick	1000	With Fins Your Choice
Pull	1000	No Fins Your Choice
Swim	20x50	Freestyle, No Fins
Swim	20x50	Breaststroke

Week Twelve – Sunday – Weights

Session Four

- Seated Rows
- Bench Press
- Bend Over Rows
- Machine Push Aparts
- Cleans
- Hamstrings
- 15min. Bike

NOTES TO WEEK TWELVE SCHEDULES

Anaerobic schedules are programmed on Monday, Wednesday and Saturday. A number of well-respected coaches feel anaerobic training should be limited to two sessions per week. There is sense in this view. It is preferable to be short of anaerobic conditioning than have done too much. Three anaerobic sessions however can be swum with more security in a Lydiard program because:

1. Concentrated anaerobic training is restricted to just four weeks.
2. The sessions are swum in a very disciplined and restrained manner.
3. The Lydiard emphasis on establishing a large base of aerobic conditioning equips the swimmer to handle anaerobic stress better than other methods of training.

In the build-up, the long schedules swum in the first five weeks are repeated in the second five weeks. The same principle is applied to the anaerobic training. The anaerobic period's Week One schedules are repeated in Week Three and the Week Two schedules are repeated in Week Four (see Table on p. 143). This allows the swimmer's anaerobic adaptation to be measured through the four weeks.

The repetition distances swum in this period will vary depending on the swimmer's specialist event. The training is becoming more race specific. The repetition distances included in the sample daily schedules are for a 50m/100m swimmer. The table below shows the repetition distances recommended for all the different events. Specialists in strokes other than freestyle should swim the 100m/200m repetition distances.

ANAEROBIC SETS

50 and 100 Swimmer		
Day	Weeks	Set
Monday	12&14	6x400
Wednesday	12&14	45x50
Saturday	12&14	16x150
Monday	13&15	12x200
Wednesday	13&15	32x75
Saturday	13&15	24x100

100 and 200 Swimmer		
Day	Weeks	Set
Monday	12&14	6x500
Wednesday	12&14	24x100
Saturday	12&14	8x300
Monday	13&15	6x400
Wednesday	13&15	16x150
Saturday	13&15	12x200

200 and 400 Swimmer		
Day	Weeks	Set
Monday	12&14	3x1000
Wednesday	12&14	12x200
Saturday	12&14	6x500
Monday	13&15	4x600
Wednesday	13&15	8x300
Saturday	13&15	6x400

The distances swum are selected in order to provide a wide range of anaerobic experiences. Distances are chosen that are shorter, longer and the same as the distance of the swimmer's main race. The very best anaerobic conditioning is achieved when the swimmer has to adjust to moderate anaerobic stress over longer distances and more intense stress over shorter distances. The aim is to provide a comprehensive range of aerobic and anaerobic conditioning experiences so that the athlete arrives at their competition equipped to handle their race irrespective of the competition or the way the race is swum. Whatever happens, they've experienced it all before. Whatever the distance of the individual repetitions, the total distance of each anaerobic set is kept between 2400m and 3000m.

In addition to the three anaerobic days per week there are two further specialist sessions. Hills are included on Thursday afternoon and stroke correction on Saturday afternoon. Both sessions have the same purpose and are swum the same way as in the transition week's program.

The remaining eight sessions are general aerobic swimming to maintain the swimmer's aerobic conditioning and allow time for recovery from the anaerobic swims. For example on Monday morning there is a straight 3000m swim, on Tuesday afternoon 4 x 1000m and on Friday afternoon 7 x 400m individual medleys. These must be swum as easy aerobic swims. The anaerobic training will have lowered the swimmer's blood pH and as anyone who has trained strenuously knows acidity in the blood can result in sore muscles. Gentle aerobic swimming over at least 48 hours is the best therapy for restoring a swimmer's blood levels to their normal pH. Certainly better than the day off each week advocated by many swim squads. Recovery aerobic swims should also be used to evaluate and check technique. As a swimmer speeds up and incurs the fatigue of anaerobic conditioning, faults can appear that were not evident during the slower build-up weeks.

YOUNGER AND LESS EXPERIENCED SWIMMERS

In the "pre-Lydiard" age group years, anaerobic training should be avoided. Young swimmers are not physiologically ready for the stress of anaerobic training. The physical characteristics required to benefit from this sort of training normally do not mature until the mid-teen years. But beware – you will probably be the only coach in the area that is not setting sets of eight or ten 100m and whipping the junior squads into action. To make things worse, your juniors will probably be beaten in the local McDonald's mini-Olympics. Fear not, your caution will be rewarded. When your group is eighteen, and is enjoying pushing through another week of 100 kilometers in preparation for the next World Cup meet, your neighbor will still be thrashing the next generation of ten year olds and cursing his luck that none of them have "made it" like yours have. Contrary to what most parents instinctively believe, it is not the distance swum or the early mornings that "kills-off" young swimmers – it is speed. The traffic sign you see on lots of roads around the world should be put at the end of every pool as well – "SPEED KILLS." Swimmers in their twenties, who have swum 20,000 kilometers of aerobic conditioning, can handle the anaerobic schedules in this book. Prior to this, and even if your swimmers lose races as a result, exercise great caution through the anaerobic stage.

Samantha ready to go – at 6 years of age racing and training should be varied and enjoyable.

WEEK THIRTEEN SCHEDULES

Week Thirteen – Monday AM – 6000 Mixed		
Warm-up	1000 1000	Kick, With Fins Your Choice Swim, No Fins Your Choice
Main Set	10x400	Done As Freestyle 1xSwim, 1xKick Freestyle 1xPull, 1xFly Kick Backstroke 1xSwim, 1x Kick Backstroke 1xPull, 1x Breast Kick 1xButterfly Swim With Fins 1xIndividual Medley

Week Thirteen – Monday PM – 6000 Anaerobic		
Warm-up	1000 1000	Kick, With Fins Your Choice Swim, No Fins Your Choice
Drills	500	
Swim Throughs	100	
Main Set	12x200	Done As 3x200 Freestyle 3x200 Breaststroke 3x200 Backstroke 3x200 Individual Medley Kick
Warm-down	500 500	Kick, With Fins Your Choice Swim, With Fins Your Choice

Week Thirteen – Tuesday AM – 6000 Kick			
Warm-up	1500	Swim, No Fins Your Choice	
Main Set	9x300	Kick, With Fins, Done As	2x300 Freestyle 2x300 Backstroke 2x300 Butterfly 3x300 100 Freestyle 100 Backstroke 100 Butterfly
	8x100	Swim/Kick, Done As	2x100 Kick Breast 2x100 Kick Breast 4x100 Swim Breast
Warm-down	500 500	Kick, With Fins Your Choice Swim, With Fins Your Choice	

Week Thirteen – Tuesday PM – 7000 Long			
Warm-up	1000 1000	Kick, With Fins Your Choice Swim, No Fins Your Choice	
Main Set	8x500	Done As	1) 2x Freestyle Swim 2) 1x Freestyle Pull 3) 2x Backstroke Swim 4) 1x Backstroke Pull 5) 1x Butterfly, With Fins 6) 1x Breaststroke
Warm-down	500 500	Kick, With Fins Your Choice Swim, With Fins Your Choice	

Week Thirteen – Tuesday – Weights

Session One

- Pull Down Behind
- Chin Ups
- Flies
- Wrist Curl
- Forearm Pull Downs
- Sit Ups
- 15min. Bike

Week Thirteen – Wednesday AM – 6000 Individual Medley		
Warm-up	2000	No Fins Your Choice
Main Set	5x100	Butterfly, Swim, With Fins
	200	Butterfly, Kick, No Fins
	300	Butterfly, Kick, With Fins
	5x100	Backstroke, Swim
	200	Backstroke, Kick, No Fins
	300	Backstroke, Kick, With Fins
	5x100	Breaststroke, Swim
	2x100	Delayed Breaststroke, Swim
	300	Breaststroke, Kick
	5x100	Freestyle, Swim
	200	Freestyle, Kick, No Fins
	300	Freestyle, Kick, With Fins

Week Thirteen – Wednesday PM – 6000 Anaerobic			
Warm-up	1000	Kick, With Fins Your Choice	
	1000	Swim, No Fins Your Choice	
Drills	500		
Swim Throughs	100		
Main Set	32x75	Done As	8x75 Freestyle
			8x75 Breaststroke
			6x75 Backstroke
			2x75 Butterfly
			2x75 Freestyle Kick
			2x75 Breaststroke Kick
			2x75 Backstroke Kick
			2x75 Butterfly Kick
Warm-down	500	Kick, With Fins Your Choice	
	500	Swim, With Fins Your Choice	

Week Thirteen – Wednesday – Weights

Session Two

- Pull Down Front
- Curls
- Elbow Raises
- Two Form Dips
- Back Lifts
- Squats
- 15min. Bike

Week Thirteen – Thursday AM – 7000 Kick

Set One, No Fins	1500	Backstroke Swim
Set Two, With Fins	1000	Swim, Butterfly / Butterfly Drills
	500	Freestyle Kick
	300	Backstroke Kick
	200	Butterfly Kick
Set Three, No Fins	1500	Freestyle Pull
Set Four, With Fins	1000	Swim
	500	Freestyle Kick
	300	Backstroke Kick
	200	Butterfly Kick

Week Thirteen – Thursday PM – 6000 Hills

Warm-up	1000	Kick, With Fins Your Choice
	1000	Swim, No Fins Your Choice
Drills	500	
Main Set	7x15	Breaststroke, Swim Hills
	7x15	Backstroke, Swim Hills
	7x15	Freestyle, Kick Hills
	7x15	Butterfly, Kick Hills
Warm-down	1000	Kick, With Fins Your Choice
	1000	Swim, With Fins Your Choice

Week Thirteen – Thursday – Weights

Session Three

- Pull Down Front
- Dips
- Dumb Bell Behind Head
- Machine Pull Together
- Tricep Push Downs
- Leg Raises
- 15min. Bike

Week Thirteen – Friday AM – 6000 Mixed

Warm-up	1000	Kick, With Fins Your Choice	
	1000	Swim, No Fins Your Choice	
Main Set	300	Kick, No Fins, Done As	100 Butterfly 100 Backstroke 100 Breaststroke
	8x100	Freestyle On 1.30	
	300	Swim , No Fins, Done As	100 Butterfly 100 Backstroke 100 Breaststroke
	6x100	Freestyle On 1.30	
	300	Swim, With Fins, Done As	100 Butterfly 100 Backstroke 100 Breaststroke
	4x100	Freestyle On 1.30	
	300	Swim , No Fins, Done As	100 Butterfly 100 Backstroke 100 Breaststroke
	2x100	Freestyle On 1.30	
	300	Kick, No Fins, Done As	100 Butterfly 100 Backstroke 100 Breaststroke
Warm-down	500	Swim, With Fins Your Choice	

Week Thirteen – Friday PM – 7000 Mixed

Warm-up	1000	Swim, No Fins Your Choice		
	500	Pull, No Fins Your Choice		
	500	Kick With Fins Your Choice		
Drills	500	Normal		
Main Set	400 Free	200 IM	100 Fly	50 Fly/Back
	400 Free	200 IM	100 Back	50 Back/Breast
	400 Free	200 IM	100 Breast	50 Breast/Free
	400 Free	200 IM	100 Free	50 Free/Fly
Warm-down	500	Kick, No Fins, Include 100 Breaststroke Kick		
	500	Kick, With Fins Your Choice		
	500	Swim, With Fins Your Choice		

Week Thirteen – Friday – Weights

Session Four

- Seated Rows
- Bench Press
- Bend Over Rows
- Machine Push Aparts
- Cleans
- Hamstrings
- 15min. Bike

Week Thirteen – Saturday AM – 6000 Anaerobic			
Warm-up	1000	Kick, With Fins Your Choice	
	1000	Swim, No Fins Your Choice	
Drills	500		
Swim Throughs	100		
Main Set	24x100	Done As	5x100 Freestyle
			5x100 Breaststroke
			5x100 Backstroke
			5x100 Individual Medley
			1x100 Freestyle Kick
			1x100 Breaststroke Kick
			1x100 Backstroke Kick
			1x100 Butterfly Kick
Warm-down	500	Kick, With Fins Your Choice	
	500	Swim, With Fins Your Choice	

Week Thirteen – Saturday PM – 5000 Stroke Correction			
Warm-up	1000	Kick, With Fins Your Choice	
	1000	Swim, No Fins Your Choice	
Drills	500		
Main Set	800	Stroke Correction	
Kick	3x400	With Fins, Done As	1) Freestyle
			2) Backstroke
			3) Butterfly
Kick	500	Breaststroke	

Week Thirteen – Sunday AM – 6000 Mixed		
Swim	2000	No Fins Your Choice
Kick	1000	With Fins Your Choice
Pull	1000	No Fins Your Choice
Swim	20x50	Butterfly , With Fins Your Choice
Swim	20x50	Backstroke, No Fins

Week Thirteen – Sunday – Weights

Session One

- Pull Down Behind
- Chin Ups
- Flies
- Wrist Curl
- Forearm Pull Downs
- Sit Ups
- 15min. Bike

NOTES TO WEEK THIRTEEN SCHEDULES

The way the anaerobic sets are swum is critical to their effectiveness. Most squads and coaches are aware of the principle at work – that the more arduous the exercise, the more lactic acid accumulates in the muscles and diffuses into the blood stream. Performance declines once the amount of blood lactate reaches a certain level. "If that's the case," says the logic of many coaches," the more arduous the training schedule, the more lactic acid accumulates, the better." I've seen some amazing schedules written in the belief that harder is better. Toni Jeffs read an anaerobic schedule written on the white board at a national training camp once and walked out. I thought she was right, the schedule was horrendous, so was trying to explain where she had gone.

Lydiard's program does not view anaerobic training this way. The swimmer's metabolism has to be stressed in a sufficiently controlled manner that the very highest levels of lactic acid are accumulated throughout the body. Crashing into a flat out set of 100m will not do this. All that happens then is that large amounts of lactic acid build up in the muscles which seize up before the lactic acid has had time to diffuse in any significant way into the blood system. In our program, each set is 2400m to 3000m long, irrespective of the length of each repetition. This means the sets will take 25 to 30 minutes of actual swimming time to complete. This is important, very important. The swimmer must swim as strongly as he or she can, but must last the full 2400m and the full 30 minutes. Go faster and lactic acid will seize up the muscles before diffusing fully into all parts of the blood stream, go slower and lactic acid will not accumulate sufficiently to provide the desired training benefit. In summary, anaerobic sets must be swum at a speed that the swimmer can keep going for 30 minutes of actual swimming time. Completely stuffed, but only at the end of 30 minutes, is the instruction.

This is why Lydiard never worried whether anaerobic sets were run on a track or the road or a golf course. Lydiard got New Zealand's 1974 Commonwealth Games 10,000m champion, Dick Taylor, to do most of his anaerobic training by running the various length fairways at the local golf course as fast as he could for 30 minutes.

The other thing Lydiard never worried about was timing these sets. One of the real problems with swimming training is it always takes place between concrete walls, an exact distance apart. The temptation to time everything is overwhelming. With an exact distance, and an exact time, and an exact heart rate, and a pH monitor, and a book of mathematical tables your average swimming coach can predict the next coming of Christ. I'm forever falling into the same trap. We all need to be more relaxed. As long as the swimmer is going as hard as possible for 30 minutes for about the number of repetitions planned, the physiological adaptations expected will occur.

It is important the coach teaches the swimmer that an anaerobic session is all about achieving the required lactated state. If the swimmer starts off too fast and tires too soon, then he or she should stop. Pushing on when the purpose of the session has already been accomplished is possibly doing damage. Similarly, if the swimmer reaches the end of the set in 30 minutes and is not fully fatigued, the session should be extended until the swimmer feels the purpose of the session has been accomplished. How you feel, is as good a measure as any heart rate monitor, lactate test or (even) stop watch. In fact studies at the International Center For Aquatic Research determined that "training performance can be accounted for by using perceived exertion. Perceived exertion correlates well with established categories of work and can be an effective and accurate method of having swimmers train more specifically for their event requirements." So there you have it – how you feel works.

YOUNGER AND LESS EXPERIENCED SWIMMERS

As we have already noted, young swimmers need to treat the anaerobic weeks with even greater caution than experienced swimmers. They do not have the reserves of aerobic conditioning that provide some protection to older athletes. Nor do they have the knowledge of how to swim the programs. I tell my novice swimmers that while the speed they swim the anaerobic swims should be faster than their aerobic conditioning, they must not end the session in a state of collapsed exhaustion. I stress the importance of not going too fast. This can often end up with younger swimmers completing the four weeks of anaerobic training still not fully anaerobically fit. Better that than overtraining the novice swimmer.

In addition to maintaining a close watch on the effort used in this training, it is proper to reduce the distance of the anaerobic sets for young swimmers – but keep in mind the 30 minute rule. While experienced swimmers will swim six or seven 400m in 30 minutes swimming time, less experienced swimmers might manage only 6 x 300m in the same time. In that case that is what they should do. Each of the six anaerobic sets can be adjusted in a similar manner. For example I reduce the 16x150m by making the set (1x150m-1x75m)x8 and changing the 12x200m into (1x200-1x100)x6. It is not difficult to adjust all the anaerobic sets in a similar manner. When Jane Copland was starting out, I used to get her to do the 100m program by swimming one 100m followed by a 50m, followed by a 100m through to the full 30 minutes. As her swimming improved some of the 50m became 100m until she was doing the whole set as 100m. The principle is that inexperienced swimmers should reduce the distance swum to accommodate their ability level but must stick to the 30 minutes rule.

Week Fourteen – Monday AM – 6000 Mixed		
Warm-up	1000	Kick, With Fins Your Choice
	1000	Swim, No Fins Your Choice
Main Set	3x1000	Done As 1x Freestyle Swim
		1x Individual Medley Kick
		1x Backstroke Swim
Warm-down	500	Kick, With Fins Your Choice
	500	Swim, With Fins Your Choice

Week Fourteen – Monday PM – 6000 Anaerobic		
Warm-up	1000	Kick, With Fins Your Choice
	1000	Swim, No Fins Your Choice
Drills	500	
Swim Throughs	100	
Main Set	6x400	Done As 2x400 Freestyle
		1x400 Breaststroke
		1x400 Backstroke
		1x400 Individual Medley Swim
		1x400 Individual Medley Kick
Warm-down	500	Kick, With Fins Your Choice
	500	Swim, With Fins Your Choice

Week Fourteen – Tuesday AM – 6000 Kick			
Warm-up	1000	Swim, No Fins Your Choice	
Main Set	4x300	Kick, With Fins, Done As	1x100 Freestyle 1x100 Backstroke 1x100 Butterfly
	6x300	Kick, With Fins, Done As	2x300 Freestyle 2x300 Backstroke 2x300 Butterfly
	1000	Kick, No Fins, Done As	Individual Medley
Warm-down	1000	Swim, No Fins Your Choice	

Week Fourteen – Tuesday PM – 7000 Long			
Warm-up	1000 1000	Kick, With Fins Your Choice Swim, No Fins Your Choice	
Main Set	2x2000	Done As	1) Freestyle Swim 2) Backstroke Swim
Warm-down	500 500	Kick, With Fins Your Choice Swim, With Fins Your Choice	

Week Fourteen – Tuesday – Weights

Session Two

- Pull Down Front
- Curls
- Elbow Raises
- Two Form Dips
- Back Lifts
- Squats
- 15min. Bike

Week Fourteen – Wednesday AM – 6000 Individual Medley		
Set One, No Fins	1000	Freestyle, Swim
	700	Backstroke, Swim
	200	Breaststroke, Swim
	100	Breaststroke, Kick
Set Two, With Fins	700	Freestyle, Kick
	200	Backstroke, Kick
	100	Butterfly, Kick
Set Three, No Fins	700	Backstroke, Pull
	200	Breaststroke, Swim
	100	Breaststroke, Kick
Set Four, With Fins	1000	Individual Medley
	700	Freestyle, Kick
	200	Backstroke, Kick
	100	Butterfly, Kick

Week Fourteen – Wednesday PM – 6000 Anaerobic		
Warm-up	1000	Kick, With Fins Your Choice
	1000	Swim, No Fins Your Choice
Drills	500	
Swim Throughs	100	
Main Set	45x50	Done As 10x50 Freestyle
		10x50 Breaststroke
		10x50 Backstroke
		3x50 Butterfly
		3x50 Freestyle Kick
		3x50 Breaststroke Kick
		3x50 Backstroke Kick
		3x50 Butterfly Kick
Warm-down	500	Kick, With Fins Your Choice
	500	Swim, With Fins Your Choice

Week Fourteen – Wednesday – Weights

Session Three

- Pull Down Front
- Dips
- Dumb Bell Behind Head
- Machine Pull Together
- Tricep Push Downs
- Leg Raises
- 15min. Bike

Week Fourteen – Thursday AM – 7000 Kick

Warm-up	1400	Kick, With Fins Your Choice	
Main Set	5x200	Swim, No Fins, Done As	1x Butterfly 1x Backstroke 1x Breaststroke 1x Freestyle 1x Individual Medley
	1000	Kick, With Fins Your Choice	
	200	Kick, Breaststroke No Fins	
	100	Kick, Butterfly No Fins	
	10x100	Swim, No Fins, Freestyle	
	1000	Kick, With Fins Your Choice	
	200	Kick, Freestyle No Fins	
	100	Kick, Backstroke No Fins	
	20x50	Swim, 5xEach Stroke	

Week Fourteen – Thursday PM – 6000 Hills

Warm-up	1000	Kick, With Fins Your Choice
	1000	Swim, No Fins Your Choice
Drills	500	
Main Set	7x15	Freestyle Swim Hills
	7x15	Butterfly Swim Hills
	7x15	Breaststroke Kick Hills
	7x15	Backstroke Kick Hills
Warm-down	1000	Kick, With Fins Your Choice
	1000	Swim, With Fins Your Choice

Week Fourteen – Thursday – Weights

Session Four

- Seated Rows
- Bench Press
- Bend Over Rows
- Machine Push Aparts
- Cleans
- Hamstrings
- 15min. Bike

Week Fourteen – Friday AM – 6000 Mixed

Warm-up	1000	Kick, With Fins Your Choice	
	1000	Swim, No Fins Your Choice	
Main Set	5x200	Swim	5x Individual Medley
			5x Breaststroke
	1000	Kick, Done As	800 With Fins Your Choice
			200 Breaststroke Kick
		10x100 Swim	5x Individual Medley
			5x Breaststroke
Warm-down	500	Kick, With Fins Your Choice	
	500	Swim, With Fins Your Choice	

Week Fourteen – Friday PM – 7000 Mixed

Warm-up	1000	Kick, With Fins Your Choice	
	1000	Swim, No Fins Your Choice	
Drills	200	Backstroke and Breaststroke Only	
Main Set	7x400	Done As	1) 400 Individual Medley
			2) 100 IM/50Fly/50Back
			100IM/50Breast/50Fr
			3) 400 Freestyle Pull
			4) 100IM/50Fly/50Back
			100IM/50Breast/50Fr
			5) 400 Individual Medley
			6) 100IM/50Fly/50Back
			100IM/50Breast/50Fr
			7) 400 Freestyle Pull
Warm-down	1000	Kick, With Fins Your Choice	
	1000	Swim, With Fins Your Choice	

Week Fourteen – Friday – Weights

Session One

- Pull Down Behind
- Chin Ups
- Flies
- Wrist Curl
- Forearm Pull Downs
- Sit Ups
- 15min. Bike

Week Fourteen – Saturday AM – 6000 Anaerobic

Warm-up	1000	Kick, With Fins Your Choice	
	1000	Swim, No Fins Your Choice	
Drills	500		
Swim Throughs	100		
Main Set	16x150	Done As	4x150 Freestyle
			4x150 Breaststroke
			3x150 Backstroke
			1x150 Butterfly
			1x150 Freestyle Kick
			1x150 Breaststroke Kick
			1x150 Backstroke Kick
			1x150 Butterfly Kick
Warm-down	500	Kick, With Fins Your Choice	
	500	Swim, With Fins Your Choice	

Week Fourteen – Saturday PM – 5000 Stroke Correction

Warm-up	1000	Kick, With Fins Your Choice	
	1000	Swim, No Fins Your Choice	
Drills	500		
Main Set	800	Stroke Correction	
Kick	3x400	With Fins, Done As	1) Freestyle
			2) Backstroke
			3) Butterfly
Kick	500	Breaststroke	

Week Fourteen – Sunday AM – 6000 Mixed		
Swim	2000	No Fins Your Choice
Kick	1000	With Fins Your Choice
Pull	1000	No Fins Your Choice
Swim	20x50	Freestyle, No Fins
Swim	20x50	Breaststroke

Week Fourteen – Sunday – Weights

Session Two

- Pull Down Front
- Curls
- Elbow Raises
- Two Form Dips
- Back Lifts
- Squats
- 15min. Bike

NOTES TO WEEK FOURTEEN SCHEDULES

Wishing swimming times could be ignored and actually ignoring them are two entirely different things. I've always ended up timing the anaerobic sets. The table opposite shows the anaerobic freestyle times swum by Jane Copland in the six seasons, from the season she began training. All the times are short course meters and are recorded from a wall push-off. The times are shown as an illustration of the anaerobic improvement that takes place in these formative years.

JANE COPLAND – ANAEROBIC FREESTYLE SET TIMES

	SET	SET	SET	SET	SET	SET
Session	6x400	45x50	16x150	12x200	32x75	24x100
1	5.09.80	36.00	1.47.33	2.27.00	52.33	–
2	4.52.14	32.04	1.46.50	2.26.25	52.48	–
3	4.45.33	31.61	1.44.67	2.23.00	49.37	1.11.75
4	4.42.50	30.43	1.43.13	2.24.63	50.63	1.09.38
5	4.38.00	29.64	1.42.00	2.19.83	48.88	1.10.00
6	4.35.52	29.45	1.39.50	2.13.00	47.88	1.07.86

In addition to the swim sets, each anaerobic session includes a kick set. As noted previously, a strong kick and fit legs are very important in achieving good competitive results. The lactate tolerance of a swimmer's legs needs to be trained in just the same way as the more obvious muscles in the back, shoulders and arms. It would be a serious mistake to swim anaerobic sets and miss out the kick sets. Do this and the swimmer's race results will be poor. Leg muscles will lactate out part way through their race and the arms, back and shoulders will soon follow as they struggle to compensate for the dead and hurting legs dragging behind them. One of the main changes to the program since I began coaching Toni Jeffs and Nichola Chellingworth is a greater emphasis on kick training. It was actually one of Australia's leading coaches, Peter Freaney from Canberra, who said I wasn't spending enough time on this aspect of a swimmer's training. He picked it up from just watching Toni and Nichola race, which was a bit disturbing. I increased the leg training and they raced better. Just four weeks after improving Nichola's leg training, she set the New Zealand 13 years 50m freestyle record that still stands today.

It is important that swimmer's anaerobic times are read and understood correctly. Not every session will be an improvement on the previous session. Not even every season will be an improvement. Most will but there are some where a full season goes by with no improvement. When this occurs there is no reason for concern. Many factors can influence a swimmer's rate of progress. The swimmer had a cold this season, but was feeling really great last season. The pool was crowded this season, but empty last season. Most important of all, however, swimmers from time to time need to consolidate their progress. Two or three seasons of good progress go by and for no obvious reason there is a season where the swimmer seems to be drawing breath, gathering reserves and getting ready to go again. I've no evidence for all this except that progress with Toni Jeffs, Nichola Chellingworth and Jane Copland seemed to work that way. Certainly progress was not a series of neat 3% annual improvements to national swimming honors. When a pause in progress does occur, be patient. Take the long-term view. Because the method of training you are using is sound, move on and it will come right.

To illustrate the point further set out below is the percentage annual improvement in Jane Copland's competition times from the age of 12 to 18. Competition times are different from anaerobic training times but the trend makes the point. The table shows that after two early big improvements Jane then went through four years of good improvement, plateau, good improvement and plateau. This trend seems quite common in developing swimmers.

Jane Copland – Competition Time Improvement

YEAR	PER ANNUM % IMPROVEMENT
1	10.03
2	4.01
3	0.42
4	2.79
5	0.76
6	2.36

YOUNGER AND LESS EXPERIENCED SWIMMERS

Both novice and international triathletes should stay aerobic during the triathlon swim. A triathlete's preparation should reflect this feature by reducing the anaerobic, and trials and coordination content of the competitive pool swimmer's program. As you know, the full swimming program involves ten weeks build-up, one week transition, four weeks anaerobic and ten weeks trials and coordination training. A triathlete should change this six months, 25-week mix to 18 weeks build-up, two weeks transition and five weeks trials and coordination. The principal feature of this timetable is the exclusion of the competitive pool swimmer's anaerobic schedules in favor of twice the aerobic build-up. This simply reflects the priorities and nature of the event. The two weeks transition and five weeks of trials and coordination provide ample anaerobic training for the swimming portion of a triathlon.

The first triathlete I assisted with his swimming training was Mr. Bob Loan, a well-known New Zealand Master triathlete. He had qualified for the 1998 World Age Group Triathlon Championships in Montreal. I coached him as I would a 1500m pool swimmer. At Montreal he swam the 1500m really well but ran out of puff, as they say, in the latter part of the bike and in the run. There is no question that the anaerobic and speed work we had done had prepared Bob to swim a great 1500m, and that's what he did. Don't make the same mistake. Prepare for the triathlon swim recognizing what it is – the first third of a much longer race.

The Triathlon swim requires the athlete's best aerobic effort. Anaerobic effort is best reserved for the running and cycling stages.

WEEK FIFTEEN SCHEDULES

Week Fifteen – Monday AM – 6000 Mixed			
Warm-up	1000	Kick, With Fins Your Choice	
	1000	Swim, No Fins Your Choice	
Main Set	20x200	Done As	3x Freestyle Swim 3x Freestyle Pull 1x Freestyle Kick 3x Backstroke Swim 3x Backstroke Pull 1x Backstroke Kick 1x Breaststroke Swim 1x Breaststroke Kick 1x Butterfly Swim With Fins 1x Individual Medley Swim 2x Individual Medley Kick

Week Fifteen – Monday PM – 6000 Anaerobic			
Warm-up	1000	Kick, With Fins Your Choice	
	1000	Swim, No Fins Your Choice	
Drills	500		
Swim Throughs	100		
Main Set	12x200	Done As	3x200 Freestyle 3x200 Breaststroke 3x200 Backstroke 3x200 Individual Medley Kick
Warm-down	500	Kick, With Fins Your Choice	
	500	Swim, With Fins Your Choice	

Week Fifteen – Tuesday AM – 6000 Kick			
Warm-up	1500	Swim, No Fins Your Choice	
Main Set	9x300	Kick, With Fins, Done As	2x300 Freestyle 2x300 Backstroke 2x300 Butterfly 3x300 100 Freestyle 100 Backstroke 100 Butterfly
	8x100	Swim/Kick, Done As	2x100 Kick Breast 2x100 Swim Free 4x100 Swim, Breast
Warm-down	500 500	Kick, With Fins Your Choice Swim, With Fins Your Choice	

Week Fifteen – Tuesday PM – 7000 Long			
Warm-up	1000 1000	Kick, With Fins Your Choice Swim, No Fins Your Choice	
Main Set	10x400	Done As	1) 2x Freestyle Swim 2) 1x Freestyle Pull 3) 2x Backstroke Swim 4) 1x Backstroke Pull 5) 2x Individual Medley 6) 1x Breaststroke 7) 1x Butterfly With Fins
Warm-down	500 500	Kick, With Fins Your Choice Swim, With Fins Your Choice	

Week Fifteen – Tuesday – Weights

Session Three

- Pull Down Front
- Dips
- Dumb Bell Behind Head
- Machine Pull Together
- Tricep Push Downs
- Leg Raises
- 15min. Bike

Week Fifteen – Wednesday AM – 6000 Individual Medley		
Warm-up	2000	No Fins Your Choice
Main Set	5x100	Butterfly, Swim, With Fins
	200	Butterfly, Kick, No Fins
	300	Butterfly, Kick, With Fins
	5x100	Backstroke, Swim
	200	Backstroke, Kick, No Fins
	300	Backstroke, Kick, With Fins
	5x100	Breaststroke, Swim
	2x100	Delayed Breaststroke, Swim
	300	Breaststroke, Kick
	5x100	Freestyle, Swim
	200	Freestyle, Kick, No Fins
	300	Freestyle, Kick, With Fins

Week Fifteen – Wednesday PM – 6000 Anaerobic		
Warm-up	1000	Kick, With Fins Your Choice
	1000	Swim, No Fins Your Choice
Drills	500	
Swim Throughs	100	
Main Set	32x75	Done As 8x75 Freestyle
		8x75 Breaststroke
		6x75 Backstroke
		2x75 Butterfly
		2x75 Freestyle Kick
		2x75 Breaststroke Kick
		2x75 Backstroke Kick
		2x75 Butterfly Kick
Warm-down	500	Kick, With Fins Your Choice
	500	Swim, With Fins Your Choice

Week Fifteen – Wednesday – Weights

Session Four

- Seated Rows
- Bench Press
- Bend Over Rows
- Machine Push Aparts
- Cleans
- Hamstrings
- 15min. Bike

Week Fifteen – Thursday AM – 7000 Kick

Set One, No Fins	1500	Backstroke, Swim
Set Two, With Fins	1000	Swim, Butterfly / Butterfly Drills
	500	Freestyle Kick
	300	Backstroke Kick
	200	Butterfly Kick
Set Three, No Fins	1500	Freestyle, Swim
Set Four, With Fins	1000	Swim
	500	Freestyle Kick
	300	Backstroke Kick
	200	Butterfly Kick

Week Fifteen – Thursday PM – 6000 Hills

Warm-up	1000	Kick, With Fins Your Choice
	1000	Swim, No Fins Your Choice
Drills	500	
Main Set	7x15	Breaststroke Swim Hills
	7x15	Backstroke Swim Hills
	7x15	Freestyle Kick Hills
	7x15	Butterfly Kick Hills
Warm-down	1000	Kick, With Fins Your Choice
	1000	Swim, With Fins Your Choice

Week Fifteen – Thursday – Weights

Session One

- Pull Down Behind
- Chin Ups
- Flies
- Wrist Curl
- Forearm Pull Downs
- Sit Ups
- 15min. Bike

Week Fifteen – Friday AM – 6000 Mixed

Warm-up	1000	Kick, With Fins Your Choice	
	1000	Swim, No Fins Your Choice	
Main Set	300	Kick, No Fins, Done As	100 Butterfly 100 Backstroke 100 Breaststroke
	8x100	Freestyle On 1.30	
	300	Swim , No Fins, Done As	100 Butterfly 100 Backstroke 100 Breaststroke
	6x100	Freestyle On 1.30	
	300	Swim, With Fins,Done As	100 Butterfly 100 Backstroke 100 Breaststroke
	4X100	Freestyle On 1.30	
	300	Swim , No Fins, Done As	100 Butterfly 100 Backstroke 100 Breaststroke
	2X100	Freestyle On 1.30	
	300	Kick, No Fins, Done As	100 Butterfly 100 Backstroke 100 Breaststroke
Warm-down	500	Swim, With Fins Your Choice	

Week Fifteen – Friday PM – 7000 Mixed

Warm-up	1000	Swim, No Fins Your Choice		
	500	Kick, With Fins Your Choice		
	500	Pull, No Fins Your Choice		
Drills	500	Normal		
Main Set	400 Free	200 IM	100 Fly	50 Fly/Back
	400 Free	200 IM	100 Back	50 Back/Breast
	400 Free	200 IM	100 Breast	50 Breast/Free
	400 Free	200 IM	100 Free	50 Free/Fly
Warm-down	500	Kick, No Fins, Include 100 Breaststroke Kick		
	500	Kick, With Fins Your Choice		
	500	Swim, With Fins Your Choice		

Week Fifteen – Friday – Weights

Session Two

- Pull Down Front
- Curls
- Elbow Raises
- Two Form Dips
- Back Lifts
- Squats
- 15min. Bike

Week Fifteen – Saturday AM – 6000 Anaerobic			
Warm-up	1000 1000	Kick, With Fins Your Choice Swim, No Fins Your Choice	
Drills	500		
Swim Throughs	100		
Main Set	24x100	Done As	5x100 Freestyle 5x100 Breaststroke 5x100 Backstroke 5x100 Individual Medley 1x100 Freestyle Kick 1x100 Breaststroke Kick 1x100 Backstroke Kick 1x100 Butterfly Kick
Warm-down	500 500	Kick, With Fins Your Choice Swim, With Fins Your Choice	

Week Fifteen – Saturday PM – 5000 Stroke Correction			
Warm-up	1000 1000	Kick, With Fins Your Choice Swim, No Fins Your Choice	
Drills	500		
Main Set	800	Stroke Correction	
Kick	3x400	With Fins, Done As	1) Freestyle 2) Backstroke 3) Butterfly
Kick	500	Breaststroke	

Week Fifteen – Sunday AM – 6000 Mixed		
Swim	2000	No Fins Your Choice
Kick	1000	With Fins Your Choice
Pull	1000	No Fins Your Choice
Swim	20x50	Butterfly, With Fins Your Choice
Swim	20x50	Backstroke, No Fins

Week Fifteen – Sunday – Weights

Session Three

- Pull Down Front
- Dips
- Dumb Bell Behind Head
- Machine Pull Together
- Tricep Push Downs
- Leg Raises
- 15min. Bike

NOTES TO WEEK FIFTEEN SCHEDULES

We have already discussed the primary purpose of the anaerobic training – to maximize the accumulation of lactic acid in order to educate the body to tolerate its effects. This is different from the swimmer's ability to access anaerobic mechanisms at a high rate. Right now we are addressing the quantity question – how much? The next trials and coordination section of the program will address the question of access quality – how fast? It is important to understand this distinction. It forms the basis for the number and variety of intervals included in these schedules. It also forms the basis for determining the rest interval between each repetition.

In most squads, the coach determines the length of rest the squad should have and then specifies a time for each repetition in the set. The amount of rest is often expressed as a ratio of the length of the repetition. In the build-up, the ratio of rest is very low, normally less than the time taken to swim the repetition. In the anaerobic quantity period the ratio of rest increases, and in the trials and coordination period of training, where the quality of anaerobic access is most important,the rest ratio increases again – sometimes as high as 1:8.

The problem with strictly controlled pace clock training is that the pace clock can't take into account how the swimmer feels. The fact that four minutes or whatever has gone by since the last repetition, may or may not mean anything in terms of the athlete's recovery. For this reason I decided to abandon the pool's pace clock. Instead I decided I would teach the swimmers what the training had to accomplish. In this case, a state of comprehensive anaerobic fatigue after 30 minutes of fast swimming. I would then leave them to determine their own rest as they swam the anaerobic set. They knew they had to rest just long enough to swim the next repetition fast enough that when all the swims were finished, they would be thoroughly fatigued. And it worked. I now almost never use the pool's pace clock. It's a prop to support coaches that are too lazy to teach their swimmers the physiology of what their swimmers are expected to achieve. Teach your swimmers well and let them get on with it as responsible adults, not slaves to a bent metal pointer spinning on the pool wall.

Whether coaches take this attitude to training or prefer the pace clock, stopwatch, everyone into the pool by 6.00am SHARP, army style control, depends, I think on their view of athletes. When I first met Lydiard, his first counsel was, "Always trust your athlete." He says the same thing today. Whether a coach accepts the advice depends, I suppose, on whether coaches see themselves as helping mature athletes achieve their goals or as instructors of children. I prefer Lydiard's way. I'm sure it makes the whole thing more rewarding for the athlete and the coach. So many good things in the sport and in life follow from respecting your athletes in the Lydiard way.

If you do decide to continue setting a pace clock interval, don't set ever more difficult times until the swimmer fails to meet one of the start times. Don't plan deliberate failure. I visited a pool in a local town recently and was told by the coach that he'd had a good day; he'd been able to set a schedule that morning that had been so tough two swimmers had vomited part way through. Anyone can do that, only someone really stupid looks on it as a victory.

Finishing Week Fifteen means swimmers have completed the aerobic build-up and the anaerobic conditioning sections of the program. They will be feeling aerobically and anaerobically fit. All they want to do is get out and start racing. And still they must be held back, just for a few more weeks. Their biggest training change is about to take place. Until now the training has been general. It has addressed the athlete's aerobic and anaerobic conditioning with not a lot of attention to the specifics of the athlete's event or competition timetable. From now on, through the trials and coordination stage, every detail of the program will focus on the specifics of racing well.

YOUNGER AND LESS EXPERIENCED SWIMMERS

If educating older, experienced swimmers to train themselves without being slaves to a pool pace clock is important, it is vital to the career development of young swimmers. You want to avoid what I came across recently in a masters group I was coaching. It was made up of very good ex-college swimmers and one ex-Olympian. It was certainly not a group for the fainthearted. On my first night with them, I put a program up and explained its physiological purpose in exactly the way I would for my experienced swimmers. They had all the information required to determine how the schedule should be swum. When I finished my explanation the group still looked puzzled. I asked, "Is everything all right?" One of them said, "What time do you want us to go on?" How sad, I thought, all my explanation of the program and how it should be swum to achieve a physiological objective was wasted. For years and at the highest levels of the sport, these guys had been coached to be robots. Well, it is my guess that the world's best swimmers in the future will not be robots. They will be swimmers who know how to swim their training, because they know its physiological purpose. A coach of young and less experienced swimmers should ensure nurturing this knowledge is as much part of their coaching as the finer points of racing starts and turns.

CHAPTER FOUR
THE TRIALS AND COORDINATION SCHEDULES

Firmly setting schedules for the ten weeks of the trials and coordination period is more difficult than the build-up or anaerobic training periods. In these weeks the coach's task is to fine-tune the athlete to peak racing condition. The motto of the period is "fresh and sharp." The hard aerobic and anaerobic conditioning work of the season has been done. It is now time to put the cutting edge on all that conditioning. This can not be accomplished if the swimmer is swimming long distances or flogging through hard sets of anaerobic repetitions at the same time.

The foundation on which the training is based is a series of time trials in the period's first five weeks and then a series of races in the period's second five weeks, culminating in the main races of the season in the tenth week. The time trials and races are consciously designed mock exams. They are tests during which the swimmer's endurance, anaerobic conditioning, speed, technique, starts, turns, stroke counts, stroke rates and all the other skills required to race well are tested and retested. Shortcomings are corrected in the week's other sessions before the swimmer is tested again. This test, correction, test, correction process continues through the 10 weeks, culminating in the season's main competition. As Lydiard said, "You should be in a good position to pass the main exam after ten weeks of mock tests." Just as important, the season's main event is a natural follow on from all that has gone before. It is something that is built up to in a logical and controlled manner. It doesn't take a coaching genius to see that this must have advantages over the traditional train-like-mad and stop-for-a-two weeks taper and hope method used by many squads.

Because of the test and correction nature of this period of training, the specific content of each training session will vary depending on the outcome of each test and the nature of the correction required. The schedules should therefore be used even more as a guide than the schedules in the previous periods. To use them best, look hard at what each schedule is attempting to achieve and then look at your own circumstance and determine whether this or some other test or correction is what you need.

The table on the next page sets out a summary of the 10 weeks trials and coordination period, showing the mileage and type of each session.

TRIALS AND COORDINATION – WEEKLY PROGRAM

Week		16	17	18	19	20	21	22	23	24	25
Mon	am	2mr	2mr	2mr	2mr	2mr	–	2mr	–	–	–
	pm	4f	4f	4sp	4sp	4sp	–	4sp	3sp	3sp	2sp
Tue	am	2mr	2mr	2mr	–	–	2mr	2mr	2mr	2mr	–
	pm	5l	5l	5l	5l	5l	–	5l	4l	4l	2hl
Wed	am	2mr	2mr	2mr	2mr	2mr	–	2mr	–	–	1r
	pm	4hl	4hl	4tt	4tt	4tt	–	4tt	3tt	3tt	1r
Thur	am	2mr	2mr	2mr	–	–	2mr	2mr	2mr	2mr	1r
	pm	4f	4f	4f	3hl	3hl	–	4f	3f	3f	1r
Fri	am	–	–	–	–	–	–	–	–	–	1r
	pm	4mr	4mr	4mr	1r	1r	–	4mr	2h	2h	1r
Sat	am	4tt	4tt	4tt	1r	1r	4mr	4tt	1r	1r	1r
	pm	3sc	3sc	3sc	1r	1r	3sc	3sc	1r	1r	1r
Sun	am	4mr	4mr	4mr	1r	1r	4mr	4mr	1r	1r	1r
	pm	–	–	–	1r	1r	–	–	1r	1r	1r
Total		40	40	40	24	24	15	40	23	23	14

Codes

mr Sessions whose main purpose is to aid recovery from harder swims. Because the main purpose is recovery, none of the swimming is hard and is broken up to include a mixture of kicking, swimming, pull and drills.

l These are sessions of long, firm aerobic swimming. In a 5km session 1km should be warm-up, 1km should be warm-down and 3km should be firm aerobic swimming of distances in excess of 500m up to 3000m.

hl "Hill" sessions of 25m repeats, with 25m easy between for technique development. Swimmers must not sprint this session. Good technique is the session's purpose.

f Fartlek, fast/slow swimming over various distances. The session is a good sharpening program.

sp Sessions emphasizing short sprints, starts and turns. Sprints should normally be 16m and never over 25m. This is a sharpening session and should not involve any anaerobic stress.

tt Sessions devoted to time trials over various distances shorter than, the same as and longer than the swimmer's main event.

r Competition race days.

sc Stroke correction session.

WEEK SIXTEEN SCHEDULES

Week Sixteen – Monday AM – 2000 Mixed		
Main Set	1500	Freestyle Swim
	500	Kick, Your Choice

Week Sixteen – Monday PM – 4000 Fartlek		
Warm-up	500	Kick, With Fins Your Choice
	500	Swim, No Fins Your Choice
Main Set	1500	Fartlek – Freestyle Swim
	1000	Fartlek – Individual Medley Kick
Warm-down	250	Kick, With Fins Your Choice
	250	Swim, With Fins Your Choice

Week Sixteen – Tuesday AM – 2000 Mixed		
Main Set	1500	Freestyle Swim
	500	Kick Your Choice

Week Sixteen – Tuesday PM – 5000 Long			
Warm-up	500	Swim, No Fins Your Choice	
	500	Kick, With Fins Your Choice	
Drills	500		
Main Set	6x400	Swim, Done As	2x Freestyle
			1x Backstroke
			1x Breaststroke
			1x Individual Medley
			1x Kick IM
Warm-down	500	Swim, With Fins Your Choice	
	500	Kick, With Fins Your Choice	

Week Sixteen – Tuesday – Weights

Session Four

- Seated Rows
- Bench Press
- Bend Over Rows
- Machine Push Aparts
- Cleans
- Hamstrings

Week Sixteen – Wednesday AM – 2000 Mixed

Main Set	1500	Freestyle Swim
	500	Kick, Your Choice

Week Sixteen – Wednesday PM – 4000 Hills

Warm-up	1000	Kick, With Fins Your Choice	
	1000	Swim, No Fins Your Choice	
Drills	500		
Swim Throughs	100		
Main Set	20xHills	Done As	2x Dives
			3x Turns Each Stroke
Warm-down	500	Kick, With Fins Your Choice	
	500	Swim, With Fins Your Choice	

Week Sixteen – Wednesday – Weights

Session One

- Pull Down Behind
- Chin Ups
- Flies
- Wrist Curl
- Forearm Pull Downs
- Sit Ups

Week Sixteen – Thursday AM – 2000 Mixed		
Main Set	1500	Freestyle Swim
	500	Kick, Your Choice

Week Sixteen – Thursday PM – 4000 Fartlek		
Warm-up	500	Kick, With Fins Your Choice
	500	Swim, No Fins Your Choice
Main Set	1500	Fartlek – Main Stroke Swim
	1000	Fartlek – Individual Medley Kick
Warm-down	250	Kick, With Fins Your Choice
	250	Swim, With Fins Your Choice

Week Sixteen – Thursday – Weights

Session Two

- Pull Down Front
- Curls
- Elbow Raises
- Two Form Dips
- Back Lifts
- Squats

Week Sixteen – Friday PM – 4000 Mixed				
Warm-up	500	Kick, With Fins Your Choice		
Main Set	400 Free	200 IM	100 Fly	50 Fly/Back
	400 Free	200 IM	100 Back	50 Back/Breast
	400 Free	200 IM	100 Breast	50 Breast/Free
	400 Free	200 IM	100 Free	50 Free/Fly
Warm-down	500	Kick, No Fins, Include 100 Breaststroke Kick		

Week Sixteen – Friday – Weights

Session Three

- Pull Down Front
- Dips
- Dumb Bell Behind Head
- Machine Pull Together
- Tricep Push Downs
- Leg Raises

Week Sixteen – Saturday AM – 4000 Time trial

Warm-up	1000	Kick, With Fins Your Choice
	1000	Swim, No Fins Your Choice
Drills	500	
Swim Throughs	100	
Main Set	200	Individual Medley Time Trial
Warm-down	500	Kick, With Fins Your Choice
	500	Swim, With Fins Your Choice

Week Sixteen – Saturday PM – 3000 Stroke Correction

Warm-up	750	Kick, With Fins Your Choice
	750	Swim, No Fins Your Choice
Drills	500	
Main Set	500	Stroke Correction
Kick	500	Breaststroke

Week Sixteen – Sunday AM – 4000 Mixed		
Swim	1000	No Fins Your Choice
Kick	1000	With Fins Your Choice
Swim	20x50	Butterfly, With Fins Your Choice
Swim	20x50	Done As 5x25 Each Stroke

Week Sixteen – Sunday – Weights

Session Four

- Seated Rows
- Bench Press
- Bend Over Rows
- Machine Push Aparts
- Cleans
- Hamstrings

NOTES TO WEEK SIXTEEN SCHEDULES

The most obvious change in the first week of trials and coordination is the drop in mileage to just 40kms. The freshening effect of a 50% cut in swimming mileage is dramatic. To many swimmers 40kms represents a good week's training. To a Lydiard swimmer it's a public holiday. Every fiber will want to go fast, to exploit new found reserves of strength and conditioning. But, for just two or three more weeks, hold back. The time to go fast is not far away. Until then just wait, wait and be patient.

The morning swims of two kilometers are wake up swims. Their purpose is to loosen the swimmer up after a night's sleep. The work of the day will be done in the afternoon session.

The fartlek session on Monday and Thursday is a swimming copy of a key sharpening session used by Arthur Lydiard and Arch Jelley. On the track it is called "50-50s", because it is done by running hard for 50m and gliding for 50m for the full distance. Alison Wright ran sessions of between 1600m and

3200m of 50-50s at this time of the season. Prior to setting the New Zealand 1000m record of 2.38.60 in Berlin, Alison was running 1600m of 50-50s in under five minutes. So her overall pace was not exactly slow. Swimmers should find their speed for the 25m fast portion of the fartlek swims improves as they begin to benefit from the freshening influence of the lower mileage. As I've said before there is no need to time the fartlek. Most of us though can't resist the temptation.

The purpose of Wednesday's Hills session changes during the trials and coordination period. The session still has an important sharpening function but it is now a session where the swimmer also drills starts and turns. The session's main set is just two dives and three turns of each stroke. Set out below is a checklist of random thoughts on starts and turns. Its purpose is to encourage coaches and swimmers to think about what they are doing and question whether improvements can be made.

1. Track starts are better than feet together starts

The New Zealand TV1 swimming expert, Antony Moss, tells everyone the opposite, but he's wrong – again. His best bit of commentary was when he announced, positively frothing with excitement, that Petria Thomas was now, "pulling her hands out of the bottom of her togs." Anyway back to track starts. If you look at the start reaction times at World Cups, World Championships and Olympic Games the track starters out-start feet together starters all the time. No evidence exists to support claims that feet together starters make up for their slow start with a better push-off. In starting, I'm afraid, slow is slow.

2. Don't lean or rock back before you dive

Years ago we all used to swing our arms in huge circles, in order to improve the distance of the dive. Then someone figured out that the improved distance of the dive never made up for the hours it took to finish the circles. Hence, no more arm swings! Leaning and rocking back is a modern version of the same fault. In starting, stay forward, go forward.

3. No jackknives or mid-air kicks

These aeronautical displays are becoming a thing of the past. In sport in general, it's amazing how often if a thing looks strange, it's probably wrong. Keep it simple is the best advice. Concentrate on simple actions done perfectly. They will produce better results than complicated dramatics.

4. Stay deep

In the old days we all tried to make our dives as shallow as possible. Everything was aimed at getting to the surface and getting going as quickly as possible. Today we know more about the resistance of water, especially the resistance of water on the surface. In breaststroke, backstroke and butterfly go deep in the dive and use that depth to get maximum advantage under the water. Because of its higher swimming speed the length of time under the water in freestyle will be less but should still not be rushed. Use the dive, don't rush the dive.

5. Tuck tight – real tight

In freestyle and backstroke tumble turns it is remarkable how many swimmers open out their turns too much. The tighter the tuck the better. The logic is simple. It takes longer to travel around a four meter arc than it does to travel a two meters arc.

6. Don't stop your feet

Many swimmers doing tumble or swivel turns place their feet on the wall and then push as two separate actions – action one, feet on the wall, action two, push off the wall. This is slow. From the time the legs first begin to straighten until the swimmer is streamlining away from the wall is one continuous process. The fact that within that process the swimmer's feet come into contact with the wall is irrelevant. The legs were pushing back before the feet came into contact with the wall and should continue just the same after contact. The whole thing must be one movement.

7. Don't stop your hands

In breaststroke and butterfly many swimmers complete each length by firmly placing their hands on the wall before removing them as quickly as possible to complete the turn and begin the next length. Once again there are two processes involved. Hands on the wall for a momentary stop, then start again with the turn and swim. This is slow. Nowhere in the Rules does it say the swimmer's hands must stop, or even be stationary. It just says they must "touch" the wall. Therefore swimmers should touch the wall with their hands in motion, sliding across the wall into the turn. The touch should only be a brush across the wall. There must be no stop, no matter how fleeting. In the year Jane Copland won her first 200m national open breaststroke title, her average turn time for

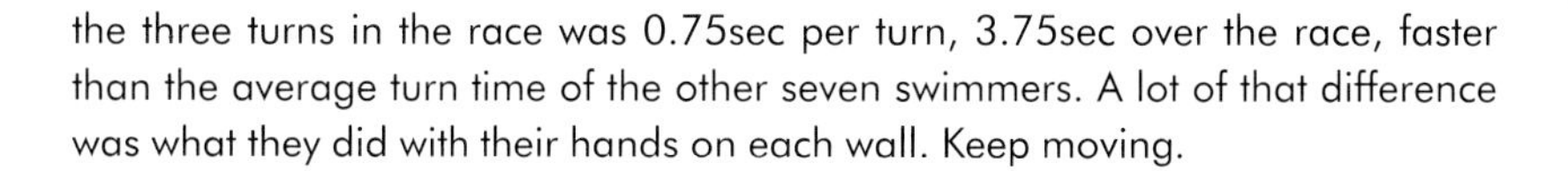
the three turns in the race was 0.75sec per turn, 3.75sec over the race, faster than the average turn time of the other seven swimmers. A lot of that difference was what they did with their hands on each wall. Keep moving.

YOUNGER AND LESS EXPERIENCED SWIMMERS

As the senior pool swimmers move into the trials and coordination weeks and as the distance they swim each week comes down, the schedules of the senior and junior members of the team will become increasingly similar. There is no reason why junior swimmers can not do the fartlek, short sprints, time trials and early morning swims characteristic of the senior program. The concessions I make to their inexperience include shortening the distance of the fartlek and warm-up and warm-down swims. Apart from that, in the trials and coordination period, experienced and inexperienced swimmers can train together. Junior swimmers will have had some experience of starts, turns, finishes, stroke technique and racing stroke plans in their "pre-Lydiard" days. They will not, however, have experienced anything like the accuracy expected at this stage – and that will take some learning.

Lolly Erickson – at 26 she began a Lydiard conditioning program as a Masters swimmer but now swims all sessions with the open squad, testament to the benefit of good aerobic conditioning.

Week Seventeen – Monday AM – 2000 Mixed		
Main Set	1500	Freestyle Swim
	500	Kick, Your Choice

Week Seventeen – Monday PM – 4000 Fartlek		
Warm-up	500	Kick, With Fins Your Choice
	500	Swim, No Fins Your Choice
Main Set	1500	Fartlek – Freestyle Swim
	1000	Fartlek – Individual Medley Kick
Warm-down	250	Kick, With Fins Your Choice
	250	Swim, With Fins Your Choice

Week Seventeen – Tuesday AM – 2000 Mixed		
Main Set	1500	Freestyle Swim
	500	Kick, Your Choice

Week Seventeen – Tuesday PM – 5000 Long			
Warm-up	500	Swim, No Fins Your Choice	
	500	Kick, With Fins Your Choice	
Drills	500		
Main Set	12x200	Swim, Done As	4x Freestyle
			2x Backstroke
			2x Breaststroke
			2x Individual Medley
			2x Kick IM
Warm-down	500	Swim, With Fins Your Choice	
	500	Kick, With Fins Your Choice	

Week Seventeen – Tuesday – Weights

Session One

- Pull Down Behind
- Chin Ups
- Flies
- Wrist Curl
- Forearm Pull Downs
- Sit Ups

Week Seventeen – Wednesday AM – 2000 Mixed

Main Set	1500	Freestyle Swim
	500	Kick, Your Choice

Week Seventeen – Wednesday PM – 4000 Hills

Warm-up	1000	Kick, With Fins Your Choice
	1000	Swim, No Fins Your Choice
Drills	500	
Swim Throughs	100	
Main Set	20xHills	Done As 2x Dives 3x Turns Each Stroke
Warm-down	500	Kick, With Fins Your Choice
	500	Swim, With Fins Your Choice

Week Seventeen – Wednesday – Weights

Session Two

- Pull Down Front
- Curls
- Elbow Raises
- Two Form Dips
- Back Lifts
- Squats

Week Seventeen – Thursday AM – 2000 Mixed		
Main Set	1500	Freestyle Swim
	500	Kick, Your Choice

Week Seventeen – Thursday PM – 4000 Fartlek		
Warm-up	500	Kick, With Fins Your Choice
	500	Swim, No Fins Your Choice
Main Set	1500	Fartlek – Main Stroke Swim
	1000	Fartlek – Individual Medley Kick
Warm-down	250	Kick, With Fins Your Choice
	250	Swim, With Fins Your Choice

Week Seventeen – Thursday – Weights

Session Three

- Pull Down Front
- Dips
- Dumb Bell Behind Head
- Machine Pull Together
- Tricep Push Downs
- Leg Raises

Week Seventeen – Friday PM – 4000 Mixed				
Warm-up	500	Kick, With Fins Your Choice		
Main Set	400 Free	200 IM	100 Fly	50 Fly/Back
	400 Free	200 IM	100 Back	50 Back/Breast
	400 Free	200 IM	100 Breast	50 Breast/Free
	400 Free	200 IM	100 Free	50 Free/Fly
Warm-down	500	Kick, No Fins, Include 100 Breaststroke Kick		

Week Seventeen – Friday – Weights

Session Four

- Seated Rows
- Bench Press
- Bend Over Rows
- Machine Push Aparts
- Cleans
- Hamstrings

Week Seventeen – Saturday AM – 4000 Time Trial

Warm-up	1000 1000	Kick, With Fins Your Choice Swim, No Fins Your Choice
Drills	500	
Swim Throughs	100	
Main Set	250	Breaststroke Time Trial
Warm-down	500 500	Kick, With Fins Your Choice Swim, With Fins Your Choice

Week Seventeen – Saturday PM – 3000 Stroke Correction

Warm-up	750 750	Kick, With Fins Your Choice Swim, No Fins Your Choice
Drills	500	
Main Set	500	Stroke Correction
Kick	500	Breaststroke

Week Seventeen – Sunday AM – 4000 Mixed		
Swim	1000	No Fins Your Choice
Kick	1000	With Fins Your Choice
Swim	20x50	Butterfly, With Fins Your Choice
Swim	20x50	Done As 5x25 Each Stroke

Week Seventeen – Sunday – Weights

Session One

- Pull Down Behind
- Chin Ups
- Flies
- Wrist Curl
- Forearm Pull Downs
- Sit Ups

NOTES TO WEEK SEVENTEEN SCHEDULES

The time trial and racing program incorporated into the trials and coordination period should be an integrated and purposeful entity in its own right. Each time trial and race through the ten weeks should constructively contribute towards the swimmer's main race in the last week of the season. The race program is as much a part of the swimmer's preparation for the season's main races as the training schedules that have lead up to this point. The strokes to be swum, the distance of each race and the number of races require just as much planning as earlier training schedules. It is amazing how often this does not happen. How often have you seen a note on the local swimming club's notice board saying, "Would swimmers please record their entries for next weeks carnival?" The coach might as well say, "And while you're at it write down the training you want to do next week as well."

We will consider now the season's time trials and races and look at the purpose and the role they play in the competitive program. The example used here is for a swimmer whose main event is 200m breaststroke. Swimmers with other main events should study the logic of the selections made in this program and choose time trials and races that make the same contribution to their event.

For example a 150m breaststroke time trial in the sample program is a 75% time trial. The same trial for a 50m specialist would be 37.5 meters, for a 100m swimmer, 75m and for a 400m swimmer, 300m. A 6x50m trial in the sample program would be 6x12.5m for a 50m swimmer, 6x25m for a 100m swimmer and 6x100m for a 400m swimmer.

The table below summarizes the complete time trial and race program for our theoretical 200m breaststroke swimmer.

WEEK	DAY	TRIAL/RACE
16	Saturday	200 Individual Medley, Time Trail
17	Saturday	250 Breaststroke, Time Trial
18	Wednesday	2x100 Breaststroke, Time Trial
18	Saturday	150 and 50 Breaststroke, Time Trial
19	Wednesday	200 (As 4x50) Breaststroke, Time Trial
19	Friday	50 Freestyle, Heat and Final, Race
19	Saturday	200 Individual Medley, Heat and Final, Race
19	Sunday	100 Freestyle, Heat and Final, Race
20	Wednesday	200 (As 8x25) Breaststroke, Time Trial
20	Friday	50 Breaststroke, Heat and Final, Race
20	Saturday	100 Breaststroke, Heat and Final, Race
20	Sunday	200 Breaststroke, Heat and Final, Race
22	Wednesday	2x100 Breaststroke, Time Trial
22	Saturday	150 and 50 Breaststroke, Time Trial
23	Wednesday	200 (As 4x50) Breaststroke, Time Trial
23	Saturday	100 Breaststroke, Heat and Final, Race
23	Sunday	200 Breaststroke, Heat and Final, Race
24	Wednesday	200 (As 8x25) Breaststroke, Time Trial
24	Saturday	200 Individual Medley, Heat and Final, Race
24	Sunday	100 Freestyle, Heat and Final, Race
25	Tuesday	50 Breaststroke, Heat and Semi, Race
25	Wednesday	200 IM Heat and Final, 50 Breast. Final, Race
25	Thursday	200 Breaststroke, Heat and Final, Race
25	Friday	100 Breaststroke, Heat and Final, Race
25	Saturday	100 Breaststroke, Final, Race
Total Program		14 Time Trials, 30 Races, 44 Total

Week 16, Saturday, 200m Individual Medley – A start up trial in an event the swimmer is good at, but is not his or her main event. If swimmers are going to make mistakes or be slower than expected it will be in these early trials. By swimming non-main events in early trials the stress to perform will be less.

Week 17, Saturday, 250m Breaststroke – Much of the swimmer's early preparation has been aimed at aerobic and anaerobic conditioning. A trial longer than the swimmer's main event will test the extent to which this has been successful.

Week 18, Wednesday, 2x100m Breaststroke – One of the 100m should be swum from a dive and the other from a turn, including the turn at the start of the swim. This is the first of the pace judgement swims, designed to replicate the number of strokes, distance per stroke and stroke rate of the swimmer's 200m race plan.

Week 18, Saturday, 150m and 50m Breaststroke – An important trial in which the swimmer attempts to swim to the 75% distance at the 200m race plan. The 50m is then done from a turn, replicating the last 50m of the 200m race plan. The rest between these swims should be about 30 seconds.

Week 19, Wednesday, 200m (As 4x50m) Breaststroke – A trial to sharpen the swimmer's race speed.

Week 19, Friday, Saturday, Sunday, 50m Freestyle, 200m Individual Medley, 100m Freestyle – The first race meet, like the first time trial, should stay away from the swimmer's specialist event. It gives the swimmer the opportunity to get back into racing mode without the stress of it being in their main event.

Week 20, Wednesday, 200m (As 8x25m) Breaststroke – A further trial to sharpen the swimmer's racing speed.

Week 20, Friday, Saturday, Sunday, 50m, 100m and 200m Breaststroke – The second race meeting should be the swimmer's first races over their specialist distance.

Week 22, Wednesday, 2x100m Breaststroke – This trial repeats the same trial done in week eighteen. It is done again now to improve on week eighteen's trial and correct any errors that appeared in week twenty's specialist event race meet.

Week 22, Saturday, 150m and 50m Breaststroke – A further Week Eighteen, repeat trial and for the same reasons.

Week 23, Wednesday, 200m (As 4x50m) Breaststroke – A further trial to sharpen the swimmer's race speed.

Week 23, Saturday, Sunday, 100m and 200m Breaststroke – The third race meeting should be the swimmer's second competition over their specialist distance.

Week 24, Wednesday, 200m (As 8x25m) Breaststroke – A further trial to sharpen the swimmer's racing speed.

Week 24, Saturday, Sunday, 200m Individual Medley, 100m Freestyle – If things have gone well in the third meet, the fourth race meet can be a further race sharpening meet in events away from the swimmer's main events. If further specialist event competition is required it can be done in this twenty-fourth week meet.

Week 25, Tuesday, Wednesday, Thursday, Friday, Saturday, 50m 100m and 200m Breaststroke and 200m Individual Medley – The season's main competition.

The total program involves 14 time trials and 30 races for a season's total of 44 race type efforts.

YOUNGER AND LESS EXPERIENCED SWIMMERS

Early in their career young swimmers can and should swim races involving different strokes and different distances. A number of times in this book I have mentioned the importance of variety in the development of young people. Race programs are no different. Once a young swimmer begins a Lydiard type training program these things change. The uninhibited approach of the young must be replaced by a carefully thought out purposeful racing program. The investment by the young swimmer in the time and effort required to swim the schedules in this book is just too great to leave the purpose of it all – racing – to chance. As soon as the training changes to a Lydiard conditioning program, the criteria for selecting a swimmer's racing program must also change. Many coaches, swimmers and parents make the mistake of mixing serious training with a laissez-faire approach to racing. This will not work. The change in preparation represented by the schedules in this book is an integrated package not a series of independent units to be accepted or rejected.

WEEK EIGHTEEN SCHEDULES

Week Eighteen – Monday AM – 2000 Mixed			
Main Set	1500	Freestyle Swim	
	500	Kick, Your Choice	

Week Eighteen – Monday PM – 4000 Hills			
Warm-up	1000	Kick, With Fins Your Choice	
	1000	Swim, No Fins Your Choice	
Drills	500		
Swim Throughs	100		
Main Set	20xHills	Done As	2x Dives
			3x Turns Each Stroke
Warm-down	500	Kick, With Fins Your Choice	
	500	Swim, With Fins Your Choice	

Week Eighteen – Tuesday AM – 2000 Mixed			
Main Set	1500	Freestyle Swim	
	500	Kick, Your Choice	

Week Eighteen – Tuesday PM – 5000 Long			
Warm-up	500	Swim, No Fins Your Choice	
	500	Kick, With Fins Your Choice	
Drills	500		
Main Set	24x100	Swim, Done As	8x Freestyle
			4x Backstroke
			4x Breaststroke
			4x Individual Medley
			4x Kick IM
Warm-down	500	Swim, With Fins Your Choice	
	500	Kick, With Fins Your Choice	

Week Eighteen – Tuesday – Weights

Session Two

- Pull Down Front
- Curls
- Elbow Raises
- Two Form Dips
- Back Lifts
- Squats

Week Eighteen – Wednesday AM – 2000 Mixed

Main Set	1500	Freestyle Swim
	500	Kick, Your Choice

Week Eighteen – Wednesday PM – 4000 Time trial

Warm-up	1000	Kick, With Fins Your Choice
	1000	Swim, No Fins Your Choice
Drills	500	
Swim Throughs	100	
Main Set	2 x 100	Breaststroke, Time Trial, One Dive, One Turn
Warm-down	750	Kick, With Fins Your Choice
	750	Swim, With Fins Your Choice

Week Eighteen – Wednesday – Weights

Session Three

- Pull Down Front
- Dips
- Dumb Bell Behind Head
- Machine Pull Together
- Tricep Push Downs
- Leg Raises

Week Eighteen – Thursday AM – 2000 Mixed		
Main Set	1500	Freestyle Swim
	500	Kick, Your Choice

Week Eighteen – Thursday PM – 4000 Fartlek		
Warm-up	500	Kick, With Fins Your Choice
	500	Swim, No Fins Your Choice
Main Set	1500	Fartlek – Freestyle Swim
	1000	Fartlek – Individual Medley Kick
Warm-down	250	Kick, With Fins Your Choice
	250	Swim, With Fins Your Choice

Week Eighteen – Thursday – Weights

Session Four

- Seated Rows
- Bench Press
- Bend Over Rows
- Machine Push Aparts
- Cleans
- Hamstrings

Week Eighteen – Friday PM – 4000 Mixed				
Warm-up	500	Kick, With Fins Your Choice		
Main Set	400 Free	200 IM	100 Fly	50 Fly/Back
	400 Free	200 IM	100 Back	50 Back/Breast
	400 Free	200 IM	100 Breast	50 Breast/Free
	400 Free	200 IM	100 Free	50 Free/Fly
Warm-down	500	Kick, No Fins, Include 100 Breaststroke Kick		

Week Eighteen – Friday – Weights

Session One

- Pull Down Behind
- Chin Ups
- Flies
- Wrist Curl
- Forearm Pull Downs
- Sit Ups

Week Eighteen – Saturday AM – 4000 Time trial

Warm-up	1000 1000	Kick, With Fins Your Choice Swim, No Fins Your Choice
Drills	500	
Swim Throughs	100	
Main Set	150 / 50	Breaststroke, Time Trial
Warm-down	500 500	Kick, With Fins Your Choice Swim, With Fins Your Choice

Week Eighteen – Saturday PM – 3000 Stroke Correction

Warm-up	750 750	Kick, With Fins Your Choice Swim, No Fins Your Choice
Drills	500	
Main Set	500	Stroke Correction
Kick	500	Breaststroke

Week Eighteen – Sunday AM – 4000 Mixed		
Swim	1000	No Fins Your Choice
Kick	1000	With Fins Your Choice
Swim	20x50	Butterfly, With Fins Your Choice
Swim	20x50	Done As 5x25 Each Stroke

Week Eighteen – Sunday – Weights

Session Two

- Pull Down Front
- Curls
- Elbow Raises
- Two Form Dips
- Back Lifts
- Squats

NOTES TO WEEK EIGHTEEN SCHEDULES

The format of Week Eighteen will be used through most of the weeks left in this training season. Its key characteristics are:

1. Short, sharp sprints on Monday to get the week off to a fast start.

2. Time trial on Wednesday.

3. Redressing errors on Thursday.

4. Time trial or race on Saturday.

Many swimmers compete week after week without having a race plan. Not a proper one anyway. A coach sitting on a deck chair telling his charges that he wants them to, "Really push along in the third lap," does not constitute a race plan. Nor does the ritual I've seen in one local club, where the swimmers lie on the clubroom floor and dream about how well they will swim their next race. They even call it dream time. When Jane Copland heard about this she, tongue-in-cheek, said, "That's different from me. I dream about how well I have already swum." A race plan is not a dream. It is a predetermined specification that provides the swimmer with all the information required to perform. As an example, set out on the next page is the race plan Jane Copland used for her 200m breaststroke New Zealand short-course record. This plan was prepared several weeks before the race. All sections of it were practiced and drilled in the trials and coordination weeks well before race day. The fartlek swims, the Hills and the time trials were all swum according to this race plan. By the time the race day arrived, executing the plan was something Jane was confident she could do. She had done all its parts, many times. She had even swum a time trial of 75% of the distance exactly according to the plan's specification. Putting it together on race day was still a challenge but it was far from an unknown challenge.

In that truth lies the key advantage of a race plan. It is a specification of items the swimmer can control. Too often swimmers are told, "You can swim 2.30 for 200m breaststroke. Go out and show them how." Apart from conveying the coach's confidence in their ability, there is no information here to help the swimmer. The end result of 2.30 is no use. The final time happens only at the end of the swim. By that time it's obviously far too late for the swimmer to do anything about fixing faults in their performance. For many years, sports psychologists have summarized this by stressing the need to focus on the process, not the outcome. The race plan provides the swimmer with the process in great detail and says, "focus on that".

All this is why I am not a great believer in inspiring pre-race pep talks. On the day of a race a coach should talk about the race only if asked a specific question. Apart from that there is no need to talk about the race at all. The weeks of working the race plan have provided the swimmer with all the information needed. A coach raving on at this late stage usually only causes confusion and worry. Information overload, just when it's needed least. Silence on the other hand provides swimmers with confidence that they have this thing under control. And they always do anyway.

JANE COPLAND RACE PLANS

JANE COPLAND 200M BREASTSTROKE/RACE PLAN OCTOBER 2001

(Time figures in seconds)

200 Breast	Start Dist	Start Time	Swim Dist	Swim Time	Strokes	Total Time	50s Time	LGTH
1	10.00	6.00	15.00	10.50	8	16.50		1
2	7.00	6.20	18.00	12.80	9	19.00	35.50	2
3	7.00	6.20	18.00	12.80	9	19.00		3
4	7.00	6.20	18.00	12.80	9	19.00	38.00	4
5	7.00	6.20	18.00	12.80	9	19.00		5
6	7.00	6.20	18.00	12.90	9	19.10	38.10	6
7	7.00	6.30	18.00	12.90	9	19.20		7
8	7.00	6.30	18.00	12.90	9	19.20	38.40	8
TOTAL						150.00 2.30.00	150.00	

JANE COPLAND 200M BREASTSTROKE/RACE ACTUAL DECEMBER 2001

(Time figures in seconds)

200 Breast	Start Dist	Start Time	Swim Dist	Swim Time	Strokes	Total Time	50s Time	LGTH
1	10.00	6.00	15.00	10.24	8	16.24		1
2	7.00	6.10	18.00	12.04	9	18.14	34.38	2
3	7.00	6.10	18.00	12.77	9	18.87		3
4	7.00	6.20	18.00	13.01	9	19.21	38.08	4
5	7.00	6.20	18.00	13.06	9	19.26		5
6	7.00	6.30	18.00	13.44	9	19.74	39.00	6
7	7.00	6.30	18.00	13.26	9	19.56		7
8	7.00	6.40	18.00	13.50	10	19.90	39.46	8
TOTAL						150.92 2.30.92	150.92	

The race plan shows the plan prepared in October 2001 for Jane Copland's attempt on the New Zealand Open Woman's 200m Breaststroke Record. The second show the result of her swim when she set the new record in Waipukurau on December 3rd 2001. As you can see she swam the first three lengths faster than planned and paid for this later in the race when she was unable to hold her planned speed. As she tired on the last length her turnover increased, her stroke length shortened and the planned number of strokes increased from nine to ten. She made it under the old record but the time would have been faster had she been closer to the plan in the first three lengths.

YOUNGER AND LESS EXPERIENCED SWIMMERS

Especially difficult for the junior swimmer in the trials and coordination period is the introduction of disciplined stroke race plans. Until now young swimmers have been used to "having a go". Dive in, go flat out, arms and legs everywhere and see what happens – and that is right and proper. But young swimmers will not explore their full potential that way. Now is the time for them to perfect the skills of the swimming trade, and foremost among these is the skill to race according to a predetermined stroke plan. It will take time and practice – probably lots of time and practice.

In the early seasons, coaches should not set impossible stroke rate plans. A top female breaststroke swimmer races through 200m breaststroke in eight or nine strokes per 25m length. Expecting a young swimmer to match this will lead to disappointment and poor results. If a young swimmer can only hold twelve or thirteen strokes then that should be the plan.

WEEK NINETEEN SCHEDULES

Week Nineteen – Monday AM – 2000 Mixed			
Main Set	1500	Freestyle Swim	
	500	Kick, Your Choice	

Week Nineteen – Monday PM – 4000 Hills			
Warm-up	1000	Kick, With Fins Your Choice	
	1000	Swim, No Fins Your Choice	
Drills	500		
Swim Throughs	100		
Main Set	20xHills	Done As 2x Dives	
		3x Turns Each Stroke	
Warm-down	500	Kick, With Fins Your Choice	
	500	Swim, With Fins Your Choice	

Week Nineteen – Tuesday PM – 5000 Long			
Warm-up	500	Swim, No Fins Your Choice	
	500	Kick, With Fins Your Choice	
Drills	500		
Main Set	6x400	Swim, Done As	2x Freestyle
			1x Backstroke
			1x Breaststroke
			1x Individual Medley
			1x Kick IM
Warm-down	500	Swim, With Fins Your Choice	
	500	Kick, With Fins Your Choice	

Week Nineteen – Tuesday – Weights

Session Three

- Pull Down Front
- Dips
- Dumb Bell Behind Head
- Machine Pull Together
- Tricep Push Downs
- Leg Raises

Week Nineteen – Wednesday AM – 2000 Mixed

Main Set	1500	Freestyle Swim
	500	Kick, Your Choice

Week Nineteen – Wednesday PM – 4000 Time Trial

Warm-up	1000	Kick, With Fins Your Choice
	1000	Swim, No Fins Your Choice
Drills	500	
Swim Throughs	100	
Main Set	200	Done As 4x50, Breaststroke, 1x Dive, 3x Turn
Warm-down	750	Kick, With Fins Your Choice
	750	Swim, With Fins Your Choice

Week Nineteen – Wednesday – Weights

Session Four

- Seated Rows
- Bench Press
- Bend Over Rows
- Machine Push Aparts
- Cleans
- Hamstrings

Week Nineteen – Thursday PM – 3000 Hills		
Warm-up	500 500	Kick, With Fins Your Choice Swim, No Fins Your Choice
Drills	500	
Swim Throughs	100	
Main Set	20xHills	Done As 2x Dives 3x Turns Each Stroke
Warm-down	500 500	Kick, With Fins Your Choice Swim, With Fins Your Choice

Week Nineteen – Thursday – Weights

Session One

- Pull Down Behind
- Chin Ups
- Flies
- Wrist Curl
- Forearm Pull Downs
- Sit Ups

Week Nineteen – Friday AM – 1000 Race	
Warm-up	Normal Race Warm-up
Competition	50 Freestyle, Heat
Warm-down	Normal Race Warm-down

Week Nineteen – Friday PM – 1000 Race	
Warm-up	Normal Race Warm-up
Competition	50 Freestyle, Final
Warm-down	Normal Race Warm-down

Week Nineteen – Saturday AM – 1000 Race	
Warm-up	Normal Race Warm-up
Competition	200 Individual Medley, Heat
Warm-down	Normal Race Warm-down

Week Nineteen – Saturday PM – 1000 Race	
Warm-up	Normal Race Warm-up
Competition	200 Individual Medley, Final
Warm-down	Normal Race Warm-down

Week Nineteen – Sunday AM – 1000 Race	
Warm-up	Normal Race Warm-up
Competition	100 Freestyle, Heat
Warm-down	Normal Race Warm-down

Week Nineteen – Sunday PM – 1000 Race	
Warm-up	Normal Race Warm-up
Competition	100 Freestyle, Final
Warm-down	Normal Race Warm-down

NOTES TO WEEK NINETEEN SCHEDULES

Finally in Week Nineteen, it's time to go racing.

I try and make the first competition a regional championship meet. In New Zealand we are fortunate that in mid-summer and mid-winter the various Regions have summer and winter provincial championships. It is possible to program two or three of these in this early competition period.

My background in track and field meant that when I went to my first swim meet I wondered what on earth I'd come across. It was an hour before the meet was due to start and the pool was full of swimmers, all stroking up and down at a hundred miles an hour. The water looked like the North Atlantic in a force ten. "What are they doing?" I asked my companion. "They're warming up." he said. I didn't understand it then and I don't understand it now. It is beyond belief the way coaches order their squads into action an hour before the meet begins and for some swimmers perhaps three hours before they race. You don't need a Level Five coaching qualification to know that a warm-up done one or two or three hours before a race is senseless. The reason for doing a warm-up is to prepare the swimmer to race. Most important in that process is lifting the swimmer's heart rate to make ready the circulation, respiration and muscular systems.

The way most swimmers do their warm-up, their heart rate, respiration and muscles will have well and truly returned to normal by race time. The only thing the warm-up has done is make the swimmer tired and settle the coach's nerves. Most warm-ups would be better described as last minute training sessions. A warm-up must be timed so that the swimmer moves relatively quickly from warm-up pool to the race start. Then the benefit of the warm-up is still with the swimmer. I recommend swimmers start their warm-up 35-45 minutes prior to their race. The warm-up swim takes 20-30 minutes, change into their racing suit takes 5-10 minutes and check in and marshaling takes the balance of 5-10 minutes.

Just as bewildering as the warm-up ritual is the parade of coaches on the side of the pool taking the warm-up, their importance accurately conveyed by the number and expense of the stopwatches hung around their necks. Two, "one hundred memory grays" and you are a knight of the coaching realm. One, "five memory black" and you're just plain old Mr. Coach, with a very long way to go.

Apart from their symbolism, I am unsure why swim coaches have all those watches at warm-up time. I have never timed a swimmer doing anything during a warm-up. Warm-up is not the time to be working out whether a swimmer is fast enough, or knows what pace to swim. If all that hasn't been sorted out long ago, the coach and the swimmer haven't been doing their job. Plying the swimmer with stopwatch information at this stage is another example of information overload. It's too much, too late and the swimmer doesn't need it. It is interesting that in years of watching some of the world's greatest runners warm up, I've never seen a coach time anything. Walker, Dixon, Quax, Ovett, Coe and Viren, I've been fortunate enough to see them all warm up and have never seen a stopwatch. Yet in swimming you can't get down the pool without dodging dozens of thrust-out arms grasping a stopwatch. My recommendation is, leave stopwatches out of the warm-up.

In swimming warm-ups, too much swimming is done too fast. This is especially true with 50m and 100m sprinters. These swimmers are best held back for as long as possible. Keep the warm-up slow, apart from one or two dives with only a couple of fast strokes. Keep away from those 15m or 25m or even worse 50m sprints. In sprinting there is one time to go fast and that's when someone in a white coat says," Take your marks, go." When I was coaching Toni Jeffs, we watched her competitors at many New Zealand Championships sprint up and down the pool in the warm-up and we knew Toni's chances of winning were improving all the time. New Zealand's National Coach, Clive Rushton suggested recently that some of my swimmers could do with slowing down their warm-up. I think he is right. It just goes to show how easy it is to get caught up in winning-the-warm-up even when you know better.

Middle and long distance swimmers appear to need a longer warm-up, including a few 15m untimed swim-throughs. The important point is that a coach's job is not to set a swimmer's warm-up. A coach has to teach swimmers what the warm-up is expected to achieve. The precise length and content of a warm-up is then best left to the swimmer to decide. Many swimmers, for example, prefer longer warm-ups at the beginning of the racing season and are happy with shorter warm-ups as the season progresses.

Coaches should avoid setting squad warm-ups as though they were a training schedule. I'm sure many of the marathon warm-ups I've seen are set by coaches wanting to impress their peers with their toughness. "I'm a tougher coach than you. Look at how far I get my swimmers to swim in their warm-up." I can't think of any other reason for the aerobic conditioning done in these pre-race swims. Peer pressure in coaching can be a wonderful stimulus to stupidity. National training camps used to be classic examples of this. Swimmers would stagger home after two weeks of putting up with a coach's determined efforts to prove he was the toughest coach in New Zealand. Those in charge had the idea that the longer a swimmer took to recover from a national training camp, the better the camp. I used to tell my swimmers, "If they are going too fast, swim at the back, but don't come home and take two months to recover." I think a few coaches have wondered how someone can race so fast who trains at the back of their camp squad all the time.

YOUNGER AND LESS EXPERIENCED SWIMMERS

Special care is needed with young swimmers in their first few Lydiard seasons. Their early races will probably be disappointing as their bodies make the final adjustment to the stress of racing. They could well loose to their anaerobic overloaded mates from the Club down the road. Even swimmers they used to beat could beat them in these early races. To a young swimmer who has just completed 1000km of hard distance conditioning this can be very depressing. Many times – more often than I care to remember – I recall swimmers saying, "I've swum further than anyone else and they all beat me." It is a coach's job to prepare young swimmers for this, to make them aware that this is part of the process. It will come right. They have laid the foundation of good things to come and must be patient while this last stage is completed.

Week Twenty Schedules

Week Twenty – Monday AM – 2000 Mixed		
Main Set	1500	Freestyle Swim
	500	Kick, Your Choice

Week Twenty – Monday PM – 4000 Hills		
Warm-up	1000	Kick, With Fins Your Choice
	1000	Swim, No Fins Your Choice
Drills	500	
Swim Throughs	100	
Main Set	20x Hills	Done As 2x Dives 3x Turns Each Stroke
Warm-down	500	Kick, With Fins Your Choice
	500	Swim, With Fins Your Choice

Week Twenty – Tuesday PM – 5000 Long			
Warm-up	1000	Kick, With Fins Your Choice	
Main Set	10x100	Swim, Done As	One Each Stroke, One Individual Medley x2
Kick	1000	Kick, With Fins Your Choice	
Main Set	20x50	5x Each Stroke	
Kick	1000	Kick, With Fins Your Choice	

Week Twenty – Tuesday – Weights

Session Two

- Pull Down Front
- Curls
- Elbow Raises
- Two Form Dips
- Back Lifts
- Squats

Week Twenty – Wednesday AM – 2000 Mixed

Main Set	1500	Freestyle Swim
	500	Kick, Your Choice

Week Twenty – Wednesday PM – 4000 Time trial

Warm-up	1000	Kick, With Fins Your Choice
	1000	Swim, No Fins Your Choice
Drills	500	
Swim Throughs	100	
Main Set	200	Done As 8x25, Breaststroke, 1x Dive, 7x Turn
Warm-down	750	Kick, With Fins Your Choice
	750	Swim, With Fins Your Choice

Week Twenty – Wednesday – Weights

Session Three

- Pull Down Front
- Dips
- Dumb Bell Behind Head
- Machine Pull Together
- Tricep Push Downs
- Leg Raises

Week Twenty – Thursday PM – 3000 Hills		
Warm-up	500 500	Kick, With Fins Your Choice Swim, No Fins Your Choice
Drills	500	
Swim Throughs	100	
Main Set	20xHills	Done As 2x Dives 3x Turns Each Stroke
Warm-down	500 500	Kick, With Fins Your Choice Swim, With Fins Your Choice

Week Twenty – Thursday – Weights

Session Four

- Seated Rows
- Bench Press
- Bend Over Rows
- Machine Push Aparts
- Cleans
- Hamstrings

Week Twenty – Friday AM – 1000 Race	
Warm-up	Normal Race Warm-up
Competition	50 Breaststroke, Heat
Warm-down	Normal Race Warm-down

Week Twenty – Friday PM – 1000 Race	
Warm-up	Normal Race Warm-up
Competition	50 Breaststroke, Final
Warm-down	Normal Race Warm-down

Week Twenty – Saturday AM – 1000 Race	
Warm-up	Normal Race Warm-up
Competition	100 Breaststroke, Heat
Warm-down	Normal Race Warm-down

Week Twenty – Saturday PM – 1000 Race	
Warm-up	Normal Race Warm-up
Competition	100 Breaststroke, Final
Warm-down	Normal Race Warm-down

Week Twenty – Sunday AM – 1000 Race	
Warm-up	Normal Race Warm-up
Competition	200 Breaststroke, Heat
Warm-down	Normal Race Warm-down

Week Twenty – Sunday PM – 1000 Race	
Warm-up	Normal Race Warm-up
Competition	200 Breaststroke, Final
Warm-down	Normal Race Warm-down

NOTES TO WEEK TWENTY SCHEDULES

Week Twenty is almost a copy of Week Nineteen. The early part of the week is spent improving the swimmer's freshness and sharpness. The time trial on Wednesday is a broken 200m at each 25m. There should be about 30 seconds rest between each 25m. The first length is done from a dive. The other seven lengths are done from a turn. This means the swimmer swims into the wall at the start of each length and is timed from the moment the hands touch the wall to begin the turn.

At the end of the week, a second weekend's competition should be programmed during which the swimmer will tackle their main events – in our example the 50m, 100m and 200m breaststroke. The swimmer's race plans will now be tested in competition conditions. It is most important not to worry if things don't go according to plan. They seldom do. In fact a perfect race in a very fast time at this stage is not the best result. You could be coming right too quickly. The main competition is still several weeks away. It is then that the perfect race in the fastest time is required. The most likely result at this early stage is that mistakes will occur. The swimmer will go out too fast and tie up badly in the final stages of the race. The race plan will be too ambitious or not ambitious enough. The swimmer will be short of speed. The dives and turns will be slow. There are more than enough things to go wrong. But keep in mind, getting things wrong is why you're swimming these early events. They are trial swims to identify errors and correct them before the main event, still some weeks away. At the time it might be difficult to keep the long-term in mind. All of us tend to panic a bit. Just remember that mistakes at this stage are not a bad thing.

If you do have a perfect trial in a very fast time it could be you are coming right too soon. In this case it is wise to ease back on some of the speed training. Instead of the sprints on Monday do a steady swim. Instead of the broken 200m time trial do some drills and steady kicks. It can be quite difficult to do this. Human nature being what it is tends to lead us to the thought that when we are swimming really fast, if we push along even harder, we'll go faster still. This is seldom the case. All that happens is that swimmers push on harder and harder until they collapse and end up run-down and tired. When this does happen it is usually too late to fix before the season's main event. In 2002 one of Jane Copland's main breaststroke competitors swam a fast time six weeks before the New Zealand National

Championships. I said to Jane, "She has just swum her National's race." I knew her coach would interpret the fast swim as a good sign and in the next six weeks would push for even more speed. At the Nationals, Jane's competitor swam a time five seconds slower than the time she had swum six weeks earlier. Jane beat her by six seconds. Good trials still need careful analysis.

The most common error in the early races is a tendency to tie up at the end of a race. The skeptics will be quick to say, "See, all that long distance training doesn't work." When they do, all they show is that they do not understand the difference between aerobic and anaerobic. When a swimmer ties up at the end of a race, it is normally a shortage of anaerobic conditioning that is the problem. This will be corrected quickly in the coming weeks as the trials, races and training further improve the swimmer's anaerobic fitness. Don't be tempted to crash into piles of anaerobic conditioning sets in training. That's what I did with Toni Jeffs prior to the Barcelona Olympic Games and look what a mess that was. Remember it takes very little to sharpen a fit body.

The same view needs to be taken of a shortage of speed, especially in the shorter 50m and 100m events. I recall the summer season after Nichola Chellingworth won the New Zealand Winter 50m freestyle Championship. Her first 50m race of the summer was the Auckland Championships. She won that too, but swam a slow time, much slower than she had finished the previous winter. Anne, her mother, was naturally upset and concerned that her daughter had swum 1200kms only to get slower. Later, at the right time, Nichola won the New Zealand summer 50m butterfly title. Early in the season, remember another expression of Arthur Lydiard's, "Anyone can coach a swimmer to win some day. A good coach can coach a swimmer to win on a specific day."

YOUNGER AND LESS EXPERIENCED SWIMMERS

Trials and coordination schedules are just as relevant to Master swimmers, surf swimmers and even recreational fitness swimmers. Most people enjoy seeing whether they have shaved a few seconds off their best time. The fastest Masters swimmer I have coached was a freestyle and backstroke sprinter from New Zealand called Iain Trousdell. He was in the 50-55 year age group and was the New Zealand Master's Champion and record holder at 50m freestyle. He had a best time of 26 high for 50m freestyle.

Iain swam pretty much the same trials and coordination schedules as the open swimmers. He did not do the morning swims but swam the afternoon training shown in this book. He was good enough that he could take on some of the "young guns" in the open squad and on a good day give them a run for their money.

The concessions to age I think are wise are for Master swimmers to visit a GP to check everything is in order before beginning time trials and the like, and watch the amount of anaerobic swimming. The combination of age plus memories of how good they used to be can lead Masters to overdo things. Start out slowly and work up gradually and I am forever amazed at the sets some of these "oldies" can manage.

Masters Swimmer Iain Trousdell swims the Trials and Coordination schedules with the open swimmers.

WEEK TWENTY-ONE SCHEDULES

Week Twenty-one – Tuesday AM – 2000 Mixed		
Main Set	1500	Freestyle Swim
	500	Kick, Your Choice

Week Twenty-one – Tuesday – Weights

Session One

- Pull Down Behind
- Chin Ups
- Flies
- Wrist Curl
- Forearm Pull Downs
- Sit Ups

Week Twenty-one – Thursday AM – 2000 Mixed		
Main Set	1500	Freestyle Swim
	500	Kick, Your Choice

Week Twenty-one – Thursday – Weights

Session Two

- Pull Down Front
- Curls
- Elbow Raises
- Two Form Dips
- Back Lifts
- Squats

Week Twenty-one – Saturday AM – 4000 Long		
Warm-up	1000	Kick, With Fins Your Choice
Main Set	10x100	Swim, Done As, One Each Stroke, One Individual Medley x2
Kick	1000	Kick, With Fins Your Choice
Main Set	20x50	5x Each Stroke

Week Twenty-one – Saturday PM – 3000 Stroke Correction		
Warm-up	750 750	Kick, With Fins Your Choice Swim, No Fins Your Choice
Drills	500	
Main Set	500	Stroke Correction
Kick	500	Breaststroke

Week Twenty-one – Sunday AM – 4000 Mixed		
Swim	1000	No Fins Your Choice
Kick	1000	With Fins Your Choice
Swim	20x50	Butterfly, With Fins Your Choice
Swim	20x50	Done As 5x25 Each Stroke

Week Twenty-one – Sunday – Weights

Session Three

- Pull Down Front
- Dips
- Dumb Bell Behind Head
- Machine Pull Together
- Tricep Push Downs
- Leg Raises

NOTES TO WEEK TWENTY-ONE SCHEDULES

Week Twenty-One is a swimming development of the Lydiard program. The week is virtually a week-off, with only two short swims during the week and a further three over the weekend. The benefits of a quiet week at this stage appeared as an unintentional byproduct of a change to Jane Copland's program two or three seasons ago. Jane had just won her first New Zealand Open Winter title and we had programmed a quiet week's holiday before she began next season's build-up. During the week we were made aware of a representative meet in Jane's local region and a World Cup Meet in Melbourne, Australia just four and five weeks away. Instead of beginning a new build-up we decided to extend Jane's racing period and enter her in these two meets. At the regional meet she set a new New Zealand Open 200m breaststroke record and at the World Cup she swam into the top eight final. Both swims were four seconds faster than she had swum at the New Zealand Championships. It was almost as if the week-off had super freshening effect. The next season I deliberately programmed a week-off four weeks out from the season's main event. The effect was the same and Jane won her first national long course title.

The explanation, I conclude, is that after 147 days of continuous training a complete and sudden break at this stage has a super compensating and freshening effect. I also remembered how often athletes and swimmers produce very fast times several weeks after a forced week-off with an injury, or a week of very light training while traveling to a distant meet. Deliberately programming such a break is completely compatible with Lydiard's doctrine of fresh and sharp. It is just taking it to a logical conclusion.

Obviously the week-off will only work when the rest of the swimmer's training has been a Lydiard type program. Many squads don't train hard enough in the first place for the break to have any effect. There is nothing to super compensate from. Other squads that save their hardest training for the weeks immediately before their main event, would be taking time off just when they normally train hardest. But in a Lydiard program it works very well indeed.

Weight training sessions in the trials and coordination period should also be based on Lydiard's principle of fresh and sharp. Their purpose should change from increasing the swimmer's strength to maintaining the strength gains made in the first 15 weeks. Strength gains from weight training are quickly lost when weights are stopped. It is important therefore to keep training in the gymnasium right up to race time. The amount of weight lifted through the trials and coordination period should reduce significantly from the maximum lifted in the build-up and anaerobic periods of training. After some time, experienced swimmers intuitively know how much to reduce the weight lifted in each exercise. Swimmers can feel when they are not straining to make each lift but are still lifting enough to maintain their strength.

To give some idea of the amount of reduction, the table below shows the maximum weight lifted by Nichola Chellingworth during the build-up and anaerobic periods and the weight she lifted in the trials and coordination period. The table is reproduced from "Swim to the Top."

TRIALS AND COORDINATION – WEIGHTS

EXERCISE	MAXIMUM KGS	T&C KGS
Lat Pull Downs	102	80
Dips	11	3
Chin Ups	10	3
Flys	17	10
Squats	200	150
Elbow Raises	46	30
Tricep Push Downs	32	20

An item of gymnasium training not discussed until now is the 15 minutes of stationary cycling that should be part of each gymnasium session. A medium level of resistance should be applied. For example, on a bike with six grades of resistance, I ask swimmers to cycle at level three. This level should reasonably closely represent the effort required to cycle along a flat to very modest sloping section of road. The swimmer should hold a heart rate effort of between 130-150bpm.

However the purpose of the five times per week cycle is not to condition the general cardio-vascular system, although any benefit in this area is more than welcome. I recommend the bike as a form of weight training for conditioning and strengthening the swimmer's legs. I have found the bike especially good for breaststroke swimmers who rely on legs for 50% to 70% of their swimming speed. In fact the reason I introduced 15 minutes on the bike into the weight program was when I went for a bike ride and noticed the discomfort in my legs was very similar to the discomfort experienced at the end of a breaststroke swim. That combined with Duncan Lang, New Zealand's best swim coach, telling me he strongly supported stationary bike work, especially for breaststroke swimmers convinced me to give it a go. It worked.

YOUNGER AND LESS EXPERIENCED SWIMMERS

The table below shows the schedules I recommend triathletes should select during the first three trials and coordination weeks.

RECOMMENDED TRIATHLETE SCHEDULE SELECTION

Schedule	Swim Session	Distance	Purpose
Time trial	Wed PM	4000	Pace Trial
Mixed	Sun AM	6000	Mixed Recovery
Time trial	Sat AM	4000	Pace Trial
Mixed	Sun AM	6000	Mixed Recovery
TOTAL	4	20000	

In the final two weeks prior to the season's main triathlon, the weekly distances should reduce to:

- 14,000m done as 4000m Mixed, 3000m Fartlek, 4000m Long, 3000m Kick
- 10,000m done as 3000m Mixed, 2000m Long, 3000m Kick, 2000m Competition.
- The final 2000m is 500m warm-up and the 1500m triathlon race.

WEEK TWENTY-TWO SCHEDULES

Week Twenty-two – Monday AM – 2000 Mixed			
Main Set	1500	Freestyle Swim	
	500	Kick, Your Choice	

Week Twenty-two – Monday PM – 4000 Hills			
Warm-up	1000	Kick, With Fins Your Choice	
	1000	Swim, No Fins Your Choice	
Drills	500		
Swim Throughs	100		
Main Set	20xHills	Done As 2x Dives	
		3x Turns Each Stroke	
Warm-down	500	Kick, With Fins Your Choice	
	500	Swim, With Fins Your Choice	

Week Twenty-two – Tuesday AM – 2000 Mixed			
Main Set	1500	Freestyle Swim	
	500	Kick, Your Choice	

Week Twenty-two – Tuesday PM – 5000 Long			
Warm-up	500	Swim, No Fins Your Choice	
	500	Kick, With Fins Your Choice	
Drills	500		
Main Set	24x100	Swim, Done As	8x Freestyle
			4x Backstroke
			4x Breaststroke
			4x Individual Medley
			4x Kick IM
Warm-down	500	Swim, With Fins Your Choice	
	500	Kick, With Fins Your Choice	

Week Twenty-two – Tuesday – Weights

Session Four

- Seated Rows
- Bench Press
- Bend Over Rows
- Machine Push Aparts
- Cleans
- Hamstrings

Week Twenty-two – Wednesday AM – 2000 Mixed

Main Set	1500	Freestyle Swim
	500	Kick, Your Choice

Week Twenty-two – Wednesday PM – 4000 Time Trial

Warm-up	1000	Kick, With Fins Your Choice
	1000	Swim, No Fins Your Choice
Drills	500	
Swim Throughs	100	
Main Set	2x100	Breaststroke, Time Trial, One Dive, One Turn
Warm-down	750	Kick, With Fins Your Choice
	750	Swim, With Fins Your Choice

Week Twenty-two – Wednesday – Weights

Session One

- Pull Down Behind
- Chin Ups
- Flies
- Wrist Curl
- Forearm Pull Downs
- Sit Ups

Week Twenty-two – Thursday AM – 2000 Mixed		
Main Set	1500	Freestyle Swim
	500	Kick, Your Choice

Week Twenty-two – Thursday PM – 4000 Fartlek		
Warm-up	750	Kick, With Fins Your Choice
	750	Swim, No Fins Your Choice
Main Set	1000	Fartlek – Freestyle Swim
	1000	Fartlek – Individual Medley Kick
Warm-down	250	Kick, With Fins Your Choice
	250	Swim, With Fins Your Choice

Week Twenty-two – Thursday – Weights

Session Two

- Pull Down Front
- Curls
- Elbow Raises
- Two Form Dips
- Back Lifts
- Squats

Week Twenty-two – Friday PM – 4000 Mixed				
Warm-up	500	Kick With Fins Your Choice		
Main Set	400 Free	200 IM	100 Fly	50 Fly/Back
	400 Free	200 IM	100 Back	50 Back/Breast
	400 Free	200 IM	100 Breast	50 Breast/Free
	400 Free	200 IM	100 Free	50 Free/Fly
Warm-down	500	Kick, No Fins, Include 100 Breaststroke Kick		

Week Twenty-two – Friday – Weights

Session Three

- Pull Down Front
- Dips
- Dumb Bell Behind Head
- Machine Pull Together
- Tricep Push Downs
- Leg Raises

Week Twenty-two – Saturday AM – 4000 Time Trial		
Warm-up	1000 1000	Kick, With Fins Your Choice Swim, No Fins Your Choice
Drills	500	
Swim Throughs	100	
Main Set	150/50	Breaststroke, Time Trial
Warm-down	500 500	Kick, With Fins Your Choice Swim, With Fins Your Choice

Week Twenty-two – Saturday PM – 3000 Stroke Correction		
Warm-up	750 750	Kick, With Fins Your Choice Swim, No Fins Your Choice
Drills	500	
Main Set	500	Stroke Correction
Kick	500	Breaststroke

Week Twenty-two – Sunday AM – 4000 Mixed		
Swim	1000	No Fins Your Choice
Kick	1000	With Fins Your Choice
Swim	20x50	Butterfly, With Fins Your Choice
Swim	20x50	Done As 5x25 Each Stroke

Week Twenty-two – Sunday – Weights

Session Four

- Seated Rows
- Bench Press
- Bend Over Rows
- Machine Push Aparts
- Cleans
- Hamstrings

NOTES TO WEEK TWENTY-TWO SCHEDULES

The week after the mid-term break is spent getting back into swimming. Training consists of steady swimming, some short sprints and time trials on Wednesday and Saturday.

Psychologically the week off serves as a period of reflection. Swimmer and coach can evaluate the results of the first two competitive outings and determine whether any fine tuning changes are required in the final weeks push to the season's main competition. By not racing in this first week back, there is time to action any necessary changes.

It could be that the swimmer still needs sharpening, in which case some extra sessions of short sprints (Hills) can be added to the program. Perhaps there are signs that the swimmer's anaerobic fitness needs further development, in which case some additional fartlek or an overdistance time trial can be included. Resist the temptation to get stuck into hard sets of 15x100m or 10x200m. They will have an effect on your race results – a bad one. Your main competitive event is not 15x100m. That sort of training is not specific enough and is too severe to be swum at this stage of the season. I know a local doctor who has a talented young daughter who is constantly being battered with anaerobic training at this stage of the season. After a brilliant first couple of seasons she is now constantly sick with glandular fever, influenza, colds and other run-down complaints. The parents appear to put it down to bad luck. They certainly never link the training to her problems. You would think someone with a medical degree would be better at diagnosis. It is amazing how many people leave their brains at the training pool door.

In Week 22 I have assumed the results of the first competitions have been in line with early season expectations and have programmed a 2x100m time trial on Wednesday and a 150m and 50m time trial on Saturday. Both are pace judgement trials. The 2x100m should be done, one from a dive and one from a turn. The 150m/50m trial tests the ability of the swimmer to get to 75% distance on schedule for the race plan time. Stress on the swimmer the importance of swimming to the race plan. Don't allow swimmers to sprint flat out and then convince themselves that they are better than they actually are. Use the trial as intended, as a test of whether swimmers can swim to the race plan. If swum accordingly and the trial comes out faster, that's good. Just don't force it.

The sample programs do not take into account the disruption caused by overseas competition. Whether it is a short flight to Australia or a major journey to compete on the European World Cup circuit, travel time and fatigue need to be taken into account when setting the swimmer's trials and coordination program. Swimmers I have trained have competed in 60 Asian, Australian or European World Cup Meets. For European meets, I program the off-week as the week's travel which allows time to get there and spend two or three days easy swimming before getting into the competitive routine. Of course, the recommended schedules have to be amended during a European tour. The normal routine of time trial on Wednesday, race on Saturday and Sunday is replaced with racing on Tuesday and Wednesday and racing again on Saturday and Sunday.

When you know your European race schedule, superimpose it on the recommended trials and coordination template of training and adjust the individual sessions accordingly. There is never any need for hard training between the racing days. Between meets, training should be steady swims with occasionally a few short sharp sprints – no anaerobic training. The races will achieve any anaerobic training purpose required to reach peak performances during the tour.

In "Swim to the Top" I discussed the importance of making sure European tours were long enough to exploit the swimmers base training. For a Lydiard conditioned athlete, a racing tour is a wonderful opportunity to swim fast times. Racing four times each week exploits the resources of conditioning accumulated as part of this program. With every race the Lydiard conditioned swimmer will get better and better. Tours of 8-12 meets over 4-6 weeks can be planned, confident that the swimmer will improve all the way through. While others are running out of steam towards the end of the tour, the well-conditioned swimmer will still be recording personal best times.

As the swimmer approaches the season's main competition, one aspect stands out. Swimming at this level requires a huge commitment of time and determination. In New Zealand, successful swimmers are allocated to a series of national squads according to their speed and in some cases their age. The main reward for being in one of the squads is the swimmer becomes eligible for national team selection. A few also get an athlete's card that entitles them to a bit of free medical attention, some elementary sports science and some sports psychology.

The problem is, all this is incredibly well meaning, but so very amateur. As far as the participants are concerned it really is just the same sport it was 50 years ago. An infrastructure of paid administrators has been put in place and are doing well for themselves. But for the swimmer in the street not a lot has changed. This problem must be addressed. The sport must be professionalized. It is a worldwide problem that each country must address in its own way.

YOUNGER AND LESS EXPERIENCED SWIMMERS

Swimming trials are an important part of triathlon training. They are the means by which athletes can practice swimming at their fastest speed, short of going anaerobic. The ideal triathlon swim is one that is as fast as possible without calling on the athlete's anaerobic reserves. Preserve this energy source until it is needed later in the race – during the cycle or the run. If your swimming build-up conditioning has been done well, you will be amply fast enough to keep up with your interval-trained competition without going anaerobic this early in the race.

For an Olympic distance triathlon, I would program the following trials in the first three weeks of the five weeks trials and coordination period:

TRIATHLON SWIMMING TIME TRIALS

Trials and Coordination – First Week

Wednesday	2000	Over distance trial
Saturday	750	Under distance trial

Trials and Coordination – Second Week

Wednesday	300	Under distance trial
Saturday	1500	Race distance trial

Trials and Coordination – Third Week

Wednesday	500	Under distance trial
Saturday	1000	Under distance trial

Week Twenty-three – Monday PM – 3000 Hills		
Warm-up	750	Kick, With Fins Your Choice
	750	Swim, No Fins Your Choice
Drills	500	
Swim Throughs	100	
Main Set	20xHills	Done As 2x Dives 3x Turns Each Stroke
Warm-down	250	Kick, With Fins Your Choice
	250	Swim, With Fins Your Choice

Week Twenty-three – Tuesday AM – 2000 Mixed		
Main Set	1500	Freestyle Swim
	500	Kick, Your Choice

Week Twenty-three – Tuesday PM – 4000 Long		
Warm-up	1000	Kick, With Fins Your Choice
Main Set	10x100	Swim, Done As, One Each Stroke, One Individual Medley x2
Kick	1000	Kick, With Fins Your Choice
Main Set	20x50	5x Each Stroke

Week Twenty-three – Tuesday – Weights

Session One

- Pull Down Behind
- Chin Ups
- Flies
- Wrist Curl
- Forearm Pull Downs
- Sit Ups

Week Twenty-three – Wednesday PM – 3000 Time trial		
Warm-up	750	Kick, With Fins Your Choice
	750	Swim, No Fins Your Choice
Drills	500	
Swim Throughs	100	
Main Set	200	Done As 4x50, Breaststroke, 1x Dive, 3x Turn
Warm-down	500	Kick, With Fins Your Choice
	500	Swim, With Fins Your Choice

Week Twenty-three – Wednesday – Weights

Session Two

- Pull Down Front
- Curls
- Elbow Raises
- Two Form Dips
- Back Lifts
- Squats

Week Twenty-three – Thursday AM – 2000 Mixed		
Main Set	1500	Freestyle Swim
	500	Kick, Your Choice

Week Twenty-three – Thursday PM – 3000 Fartlek		
Warm-up	500	Kick, With Fins Your Choice
	500	Swim, No Fins Your Choice
Drills	500	
Swim Throughs	100	
Main Set	400	Fartlek, Breaststroke
Warm-down	500	Kick, With Fins Your Choice
	500	Swim, With Fins Your Choice

Week Twenty-three – Thursday – Weights

Session Three

- Pull Down Front
- Dips
- Dumb Bell Behind Head
- Machine Pull Together
- Tricep Push Downs
- Leg Raises

Week Twenty-three – Friday PM – 2000 Hills

Warm-up	500 500	Kick, With Fins Your Choice Swim, No Fins Your Choice
Main Set	12xHills	Done As 1x Dives 2x Turns Each Stroke
Warm-down	250 250	Kick, With Fins Your Choice Swim, No Fins Your Choice

Week Twenty-three – Saturday AM – 1000 Race

Warm-up	Normal Race Warm-up
Competition	100 Breaststroke, Heat
Warm-down	Normal Race Warm-down

Week Twenty-three – Saturday PM – 1000 Race

Warm-up	Normal Race Warm-up
Competition	100 Breaststroke, Final
Warm-down	Normal Race Warm-down

Week Twenty-three – Sunday AM – 1000 Race	
Warm-up	Normal Race Warm-up
Competition	200 Breaststroke, Heat
Warm-down	Normal Race Warm-down

Week Twenty-three – Sunday PM – 1000 Race	
Warm-up	Normal Race Warm-up
Competition	200 Breaststroke, Final
Warm-down	Normal Race Warm-down

NOTES TO WEEK TWENTY-THREE SCHEDULES

Considerable thought and attention needs to be paid to planning a swimmer's race schedule. Every race should be there for a reason. There is only one acceptable reason – the race chosen contributes most to the swimmer performing best in the season's main competition. No other reason, absolutely none, should be given any weight whatsoever.

Yet, that's not the way it is in many clubs. They have several reasons for a swimmer being entered in a race. Some of the more common are:

1. To score points for the Club

This is a common motive. Swimmers enter as many races as possible to score points so their Club can beat the Club down the road for points towards some trophy. It is given legitimacy as promoting and teaching team participation. The group before the individual. The selfish interests of the individual subjugated to the benefit of the collective. Swimming Marxism.

Because the "club-first" doctrine is promoted as a moral good, challenging the concept is fraught with danger. It carries the social cost of declining military conscription. You are unpatriotic and disloyal. Your club needs you and you're wearing a white feather.

The philosophy is however fundamentally flawed. As I have said before, short of walking alone to the North Pole, swimming is the ultimate individual sport. To be successful requires being alone. Ignore that and you court failure. And there have been many failures. Search the records of your local clubs. Scores of casualties caused by the interests of the individual taking second place to the interests of their club.

National Federations encourage the vandalism by rewarding the club that scores the most points at all their competitions. The Americans make the same mistake in their NCAA competition. Swim everything for the good of the University. At least they have the good manners to pay swimmers for making the sacrifice. The Americans, with a population of 250 million, can afford the casualty rate and still find more conscripts to charge the guns. New Zealand with its population of four million does not.

2. To score points for the coach

Entering dozens of races to make the coach look good is the worst possible motive. I heard one well-known coach defend the concept by saying, "It makes them tough." No it doesn't. The training in this book makes them tough. Anyway, when was the point of competing to be tough. The point of swimming a race is to contribute towards your swimming career. It certainly is not to bring some swimming coach five points closer to proving in his own mind that he's the best coach in the district. Swimmers sacrificed all over the place, but he was the best.

It's strange that in a profession that profits most from a minimum of ego, swim coaching should have so much of it. One of Jane Copland friends calls New Zealand's big ego coaches, "The Cool Coaches." This lot engenders huge loyalty among their subjects. "My coach always thinks of what's best for me. He said it was good for me to swim eight races today. Of course, I'll swim them." Be very clear, if your coach suggests this sort of competitive program, he is not thinking of you. All he wants is the mobile phone prize that goes to the coach scoring the most points.

If I had followed this philosophy with Jane Copland, Nichola Chellingworth and Toni Jeffs, I could have won dozens of mobile phones and perhaps even a "500 memory grey". Toni was a national freestyle and butterfly champion, so was Nichola. Toni was also better than average at backstroke. Jane is a national age group medley record holder and the national open breaststroke champion and record holder. She is also the New South Wales age group backstroke champion. In many levels of competition, all three could have entered most races and would have won. However, they never were entered and the longevity of all three (34, 23 and 19 years) is evidence to the wisdom of that decision.

3. To score points for themselves

This is just as shortsighted as the other two point's objectives. Whether they are for the team, the coach or the swimmer, point's trophies are a blight on the land. They physiologically hurt swimmers and send out the message that 30 average swims are better than one good one.

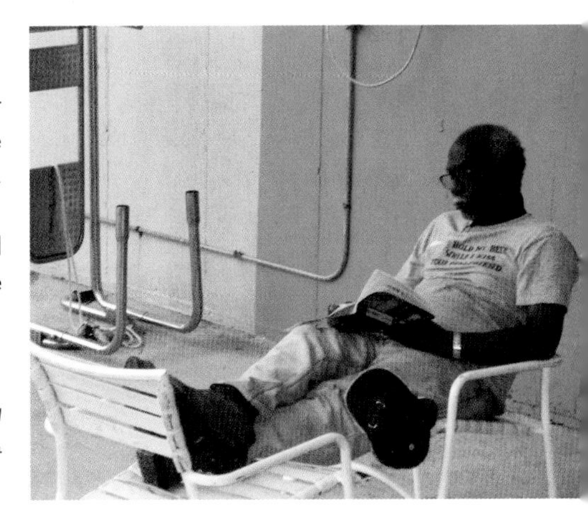

How to parent *Duvante's grandad demonstrates how to be the perfect parent at swimming practice.*

4. Because the swimmer wants to

This excuse is used often by coaches, administrators and parents to justify absurd race programs. It really is a senseless thing to say, especially when it is said by a young swimmer's parents. Parents intervene when their children might come to harm drinking, smoking or experimenting with drugs. Yet when their child is faced with the danger of a mammoth race program, "Because the swimmer wants to", it is considered a perfectly good enough excuse. Coaches, parents and administrators have a responsibility to provide guidance to swimmers. They should not abdicate that duty when it comes to deciding on a swimmer's race schedule. Then again, perhaps the real problem is that coach, parent and administrator don't want the schedule changed. They're hooked on the adrenaline rush of watching their subject race.

I do not know what the record is for the maximum number of races swum in a three-day regional championship. I have frequently seen local swimmers entered in every event (15) on the program. With heats and finals that's 30 races, plus two relays, total 32 in just three days. That's about one race every 45 minutes of competition time for three days. You don't need to be an Olympic swimming coach to know that doesn't sound right. We sit around having conferences about why young swimmers don't last in the sport. After four or five years of this sort of abuse, no wonder they want to call it quits.

5. To contribute towards the swimmer's long-term swimming development

Normally I enter a swimmer in just one event, two races, each day. In some circumstances, such as a double-up in the program, I have accepted two events, four races, in a day but never more than that. It makes sense really.

YOUNGER AND LESS EXPERIENCED SWIMMERS

During the trials and coordination period, triathletes should practice the skills specific to their sport. An important difference between pool swimming and triathlons is the open water location of triathlon competitions. This does involve different skills from the training that is the main focus of this book. I recommend triathletes always swim the time trials in open water. Trials should copy, as closely as possible, competition conditions. Attention should be paid to starting in a group, swimming in a group, rounding buoys, navigation and the transition from swim to cycle. It is particularly important to become comfortable swimming in rough water and in a wet suit. The different breathing pattern and shorter stroke required in rough conditions can quickly tire a triathlete. The word coordination is included in the name of this period because, whatever the sport, its skills need perfecting in the weeks leading up to the season's main competitions. The diverse skills required in a triathlon make this an especially important time.

WEEK TWENTY-FOUR SCHEDULES

Week Twenty-four – Monday PM – 3000 Hills		
Warm-up	750 750	Kick, With Fins Your Choice Swim, No Fins Your Choice
Drills	500	
Swim Throughs	100	
Main Set	20xHills Done As	2x Dives 3x Turns Each Stroke
Warm-down	250 250	Kick, With Fins Your Choice Swim, With Fins Your Choice

Week Twenty-four – Tuesday AM – 2000 Mixed		
Main Set	1500 500	Freestyle Swim Kick, Your Choice

Week Twenty-four – Tuesday PM – 4000 Long		
Warm-up	1000	Kick, With Fins Your Choice
Main Set	10x100	Swim, Done As, One Each Stroke, One Individual Medley x2
Kick	1000	Kick, With Fins Your Choice
Main Set	20x50	5x Each Stroke

Week Twenty-four – Tuesday – Weights

Session Four

- Seated Rows
- Bench Press
- Bend Over Rows
- Machine Push Aparts
- Cleans
- Hamstrings

Week Twenty-four – Wednesday PM – 3000 Time Trial

Warm-up	750	Kick, With Fins Your Choice
	750	Swim, No Fins Your Choice
Drills	500	
Swim Throughs	100	
Main Set	200	Done As 8x25, Breaststroke, 1x Dive, 7x Turn
Warm-down	500	Kick, With Fins Your Choice
	500	Swim, With Fins Your Choice

Week Twenty-four – Wednesday – Weights

Session One

- Pull Down Behind
- Chin Ups
- Flies
- Wrist Curl
- Forearm Pull Downs
- Sit Ups

Week Twenty-four – Thursday AM – 2000 Mixed

Main Set	1500	Freestyle Swim
	500	Kick, Your Choice

Week Twenty-four – Thursday PM – 3000 Fartlek		
Warm-up	500 500	Kick, With Fins Your Choice Swim, No Fins Your Choice
Drills	500	
Swim Throughs	100	
Main Set	400	Fartlek, Breaststroke
Warm-down	500 500	Kick, With Fins Your Choice Swim, With Fins Your Choice

Week Twenty-four – Thursday – Weights

Session Two

- Pull Down Front
- Curls
- Elbow Raises
- Two Form Dips
- Back Lifts
- Squats

Week Twenty-four – Friday PM – 2000 Hills		
Warm-up	500 500	Kick, With Fins Your Choice Swim, No Fins Your Choice
Main Set	12xHills	Done As 1x Dives 2x Turns Each Stroke
Warm-down	250 250	Kick, With Fins Your Choice Swim, No Fins Your Choice

Week Twenty-four – Saturday AM – 1000 Race		
Warm-up		Normal Race Warm-up
Competition		200 Individual Medley, Heat
Warm-down		Normal Race Warm-down

Week Twenty-four – Saturday PM – 1000 Race	
Warm-up	Normal Race Warm-up
Competition	200 Individual Medley, Final
Warm-down	Normal Race Warm-down

Week Twenty-four – Sunday AM – 1000 Race	
Warm-up	Normal Race Warm-up
Competition	100 Freestyle, Heat
Warm-down	Normal Race Warm-down

Week Twenty-four – Sunday PM – 1000 Race	
Warm-up	Normal Race Warm-up
Competition	100 Freestyle, Final
Warm-down	Normal Race Warm-down

NOTES TO WEEK TWENTY-FOUR SCHEDULES

The last week of training before the season's main competition is really a time to hold to the principles of fresh and sharp. At this stage any immoderate training will only do harm. If you are not ready to race by now, doing a crash program of training in the last week is not going to fix it. It is better to arrive at next week's competition a little short of some training item than arrive in any way overdone.

At about this time you will notice the freshening effect of the trials and coordination weeks. It is remarkable how accurate the Lydiard program is at bringing athletes to a peak at the right time. Some would say, and I have, that it is far too late for the good of the coach's nerves, but sometime during this week swimmers will just get better. Everything they swim will be faster and for no more effort. They will end up saying to themselves, "How did that happen?" It happened because a very good running coach in Auckland, New Zealand put together a program that is based on proper physiological principles and, in a judicious and logical way, brings athletes to their peak performance on a particular day.

A word of caution though. Do not try and force this peaking process. At this time of the season you will see dozens of swimmers in the pool fighting to go faster. Nichola Chellingworth used to call it "panic swimming". Do not join them. Be confident enough in your training and in the peaking process to stay relaxed and let your preparation take its natural course. It has always worked in the past and it will work for you too.

There are a few magnificent swimmers and runners who look as though every stroke and step is an aggressive painful fight. There is nothing relaxed and smooth about the way Claudia Poll swims. Brendan Foster looked as though every step would be his last. The majority of the world's best, however, appear as though they are not really trying. Popov, Thorpe, Scholander, Ovett and Snell are all athletes of this type. Alison Wright was a fine example of this quality. I've seen her run in some of the world's major meets, and she looked like it was a stroll in the park. In Berlin, in 1978, when she set the current New Zealand 1000 meters record, I didn't think she was running nearly fast enough. It looked far too easy. When it looks slow but is actually really fast, then you are in peak condition. I encourage swimmers to relax and swim this way by using expressions such as, "I don't care whether you are the fastest in next week's meet as long as you look the best." or alternatively, "Don't show me how fast you can swim, show me how well you can swim." I think most people who have know the best athletes I have helped, even those critical of their results, would say that Alison Wright, Peter Baker, Toni Jeffs, Nichola Chellingworth and Jane Copland at their best looked bloody great. And so they should, that's the result a Lydiard conditioning program is supposed to produce – smooth, easy, relaxed power.

I was never lucky enough to see Peter Snell run. If I had, I think he would have been my favorite. I did see Steve Ovett run on several occasions. At his best he was magnificent. There was the same arrogant contempt in his long relaxed stride and low slung arms that Mohammed Ali had when he danced for an opponent. You have to be good – very, very good to do that. In swimming there is Popov.

I first saw him swim in the New South Wales Championships when they were still held at the Blacktown Pool, before the days of the flash International Sydney Aquatic Center. At first I didn't know who he was. A magnificent aquatic animal was playing with the human beings beside him. How do you describe perfection? You knew straight away you were watching the model for the rest of us to copy. Since then, others have swum faster, but none ever better, not yet anyway.

And then there is Jenny Thompson. I first saw her swim in the south of France prior to the Barcelona Olympic Games. She was only doing a couple of swim-throughs with her coach Richard Quick, but I knew immediately there was no point in Toni Jeffs continuing to sprint 50m freestyle. All the training in the world and Toni could never beat that – and she never has. Thompson was too big, too fast, too strong, too good. She was a real sprinter. To this day, whenever I watch a swimmer I'm helping swim freestyle, I superimpose the mental picture I have of Jenny Thompson swimming those swim-throughs to see how close to her we're getting. Jenny's still a long way ahead – one day though.

YOUNGER AND LESS EXPERIENCED SWIMMERS

Do not swim the triathlon trials as the speed trials swum by pool swimmers. For the triathlete they are better described as pace trials – swims that the athlete uses to rehearse the controlled pace of the competition swim. There is no reason why trial swims can not be part of trials that include cycling and running. Club triathlon events can be great pace trials. Don't kill yourself trying to win them though. Remember the trials are preparation for a much bigger goal. Treat them accordingly. Even when the trial is just a swim it should always include a full transition to the bike.

There is an argument that triathletes can exclude kicks from their swimming training. Cycling and running are mainly "leg" sports and provide plenty of leg exercise. Besides, 1500m and 3000m swims do not call for a lot of kick. There is some validity in this view. The percentage of kick can be reduced by about a quarter. It would be a foolish triathlete who reduced the amount of kick by more than this or worse excluded the kick altogether. Conditioning leg muscles to the specific demands of the freestyle kick is important and can not be done by running and cycling alone. Even in triathlon swims, some kick is needed and if the legs give way, the swim will be long and slow and, more seriously, the cycle and run will be affected.

WEEK TWENTY-FIVE SCHEDULES

Week Twenty-five – Monday PM – 2000 Hills		
Warm-up	500	Kick, With Fins Your Choice
	500	Swim, No Fins Your Choice
Main Set	12x Hills	Done As 1x Dives 2x Turns Each Stroke
Warm-down	250	Kick, With Fins Your Choice
	250	Swim, No Fins Your Choice

Week Twenty-five – Monday – Weights

Session Three

- Pull Down Front
- Dips
- Dumb Bell Behind Head
- Machine Pull Together
- Tricep Push Downs
- Leg Raises

Week Twenty-five – Tuesday PM – 2000 Hills		
Warm-up	500	Kick, With Fins Your Choice
	500	Swim, No Fins Your Choice
Main Set	12x Hills	Done As 1x Dives 2x Turns Each Stroke
Warm-down	250	Kick, With Fins Your Choice
	250	Swim, No Fins Your Choice

Week Twenty-five – Wednesday AM – 1000 Race	
Warm-up	Normal Race Warm-up
Competition	50 Breaststroke, Heat
Warm-down	Normal Race Warm-down

Week Twenty-five – Wednesday PM – 1000 Race	
Warm-up	Normal Race Warm-up
Competition	50 Breaststroke, Semi Final
Warm-down	Normal Race Warm-down

Week Twenty-five – Thursday AM – 1000 Race	
Warm-up	Normal Race Warm-up
Competition	200 Individual Medley, Heat
Warm-down	Normal Race Warm-down

Week Twenty-five – Thursday PM – 1000 Race	
Warm-up	Normal Race Warm-up
Competition	200 Individual Medley, Final 50 Breaststroke, Final
Warm-down	Normal Race Warm-down

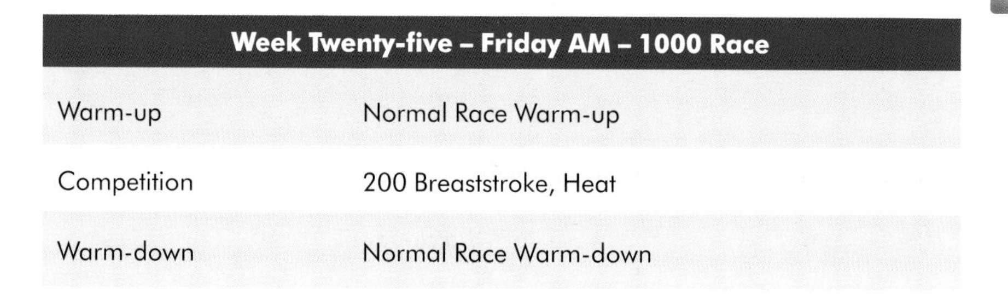

Week Twenty-five – Friday AM – 1000 Race	
Warm-up	Normal Race Warm-up
Competition	200 Breaststroke, Heat
Warm-down	Normal Race Warm-down

Week Twenty-five – Friday PM – 1000 Race	
Warm-up	Normal Race Warm-up
Competition	200 Breaststroke, Final
Warm-down	Normal Race Warm-down

Week Twenty-five – Saturday AM – 1000 Race	
Warm-up	Normal Race Warm-up
Competition	100 Breaststroke, Heat
Warm-down	Normal Race Warm-down

Week Twenty-five – Saturday PM – 1000 Race	
Warm-up	Normal Race Warm-up
Competition	100 Breaststroke, Semi Final
Warm-down	Normal Race Warm-down

Week Twenty-five – Sunday PM – 1000 Race	
Warm-up	Normal Race Warm-up
Competition	100 Breaststroke, Final
Warm-down	Normal Race Warm-down

NOTES TO WEEK TWENTY-FIVE SCHEDULES

Week 25's competition is the culmination of a season's training. If the training has been done well, the swimmer's results will be as expected. It is important to have a process in place so that the results can be evaluated rationally and without emotion. Far too many swimmers are considered good or bad by what's going on around them. "Suzy from down the road swam faster than I did. I must be no good" is not a good basis for evaluation. When Jane Copland was starting off she competed against a precocious breaststroke talent from Wellington called Gemma Davis. Gemma was very good at a young age. She set numerous New Zealand age group records. Jane swam second to her on many occasions. To evaluate either swimmer's long-term career by their results at this stage would have been a mistake. Eventually, as the effect of Jane's Lydiard conditioning took effect, Jane passed Gemma who eventually drifted out of swimming and went on to do other things. The same story could be told innumerable times with different actors. How others are doing is not a good basis for evaluating your progress – even when you are the one going fastest.

I maintain two sets of information for use in evaluating a swimmer's progress.

1. Race Record

In this file I record the final time for each race swum, the split times for each lap, the swimmer's placing and whether the swim was a personal best time (PB).

This information is important when it comes to setting future race plans. Analysis of the results can determine whether trends are present that should be addressed. Is the swimmer going out too fast and tying up at the end of the race? Is the swimmer starting too slowly? Does the swimmer start the season well, but perform poorly later in the season? Which strokes and distances are the swimmers strongest and are they changing? Resolving these matters is facilitated by the information held in the race record.

Summarizing the data also gives an interesting general view of the swimmer's career. The table below shows a summary of this data from Jane Copland's Race Record.

JANE COPLAND – RACE RECORD

Swum	Event	Number PBs	Number %
Races	430	162	37.67
Time trials	204	93	45.59
Total	634	255	40.22

2. Personal Bests Record

This is an important record of a swimmer's annual improvement. Because the data is kept on an annual basis, it includes the results of two six-month Lydiard training cycles. Key figures in the record are the per annum improvement and cumulative improvement. In Jane Copland's case, at 18 years of age she has a career cumulative improvement in the breaststroke events of 2.66% per annum. Earlier, an improvement figure of 2.96% was given for Jane's cumulative improvement. This was for all the events she has swum not just breaststroke. Experience with swimmers around the world has shown that this figure should stay above 2.5% per annum cumulatively. If it does not, progress will become just too slow to reach top international standards.

The cumulative improvement percentage figure is, of course, a consolidation of the improvement over three events, the 50m,100m and 200m, in two different length pools, 25m and 50m. Coaches and swimmers should look behind the consolidated figure to determine progress in the different distances and different strokes. It is perfectly possible for a swimmer's specialty to change. The record of personal bests helps avoid permanently branding a swimmer as only good at one thing when they may be developing potential elsewhere. Before the Olympic Games in Sydney, who would have picked the Italian freestyler Masamiliano as a winner of the 200m individual medley or the Australian butterfly swimmer Susan O'Neil as the winner of the 200m freestyle.

At the end of Week 25 the swimmer will have completed a full six-month cycle. He or she will be a much different athlete from the one that started 25 weeks ago. Most significantly the knowledge of how the body and mind respond to physical stress and improve as a result of proper conditioning will have increased beyond measure. But before starting off on the next six-month cycle of Lydiard conditioning it's time for a weeks holiday – enjoy!

YOUNGER AND LESS EXPERIENCED SWIMMERS

Several years ago I taught a young Wellington girl to swim. Her name is Kate Hevelt. She didn't like the water and for three terms of 36 lessons I tried to get her swimming. I tried everything. I was nice, horrible, kind and nasty. Nothing seemed to work. I had always been able to get young people to swim before, but I feared Kate would be my first failure. Then it happened, right at the end of Term Three she tripped in the pool, went under, came up crying but something had changed. She had felt and had recognized the water's support. We continued the lesson for another 20 minutes by which time she could lie on the water and kick a few meters. As Kate and her mother, Mary-Pat, left I said to Kate, "One day you might swim in the Olympics." At Kate's next lesson Mary-Pat said, "I wish you hadn't said that about the Olympics." "Why not?" I asked. "Because," Mary-Pat said, "Kate lay awake most of the night because Mr. Wright said she had to swim in the Olympic Games."

In spite of her inauspicious start, Kate's swimming improved until she began to swim in one or two beginner's carnivals. Her parents then transferred to Christchurch and she joined another Swimming Club. With their coaching she continued to improve. Last New Zealand Open National Championships Kate swam the finals of the women's breaststroke. What a great job Kate has done. The moral of the story though is, never prejudge anyone. You never know where the next Popov or Thompson might be hiding

CHAPTER FIVE
"NO ONE CAN GUARANTEE SUCCESS – BUT ONLY DESERVE IT"

I don't know how many readers have ever run Auckland's Waitakere Ranges circuit. I guess the answer is not many. Some fine New Zealand runners – Snell, Halberg, Walker, Quax, Magee and Dixon – became Olympic medallists on Waitakere's rugged slopes. All the physiological changes Lydiard predicted happened as these accomplished athletes worked their way around its 24-mile circuit. Their cardiovascular system improved. Their ability to run very fast aerobically was developed. Their tolerance of anaerobic stress was conditioned. Any weaknesses were harshly exposed in the long climb out of suburban Auckland to the top of the Waitakere ranges. How long did Lydiard search to find a road whose steepest kilometer is its last kilometer?

You seldom see New Zealand's best runners up there anymore. They are too busy doing track work at the Millennium Institute or sleeping in altitude tents on the North Shore. That's why Snell's 1962 800m record is still the New Zealand record. It beats me how all the sports science brains can't figure out that the Kenyans and Ethiopians don't have a Millennium Institute and they can beat us, no problem. What they do have though is a Kenyan and Ethiopian Waitakeres. The difference is they run around theirs. When we run around ours again, we'll beat them again, absolutely certain.

Besides the physical, there is the mental effect. The sheer size of the Waitakeres. The magnitude of the task Lydiard set means when you've done it there is nothing left to prove. "If I can do that, I can do anything." Out the back of the Waitakeres you feel big just being there. When Alison qualified for her first Commonwealth Games she flew back to London. As she came out of immigration, the first thing she said to me was, "Last weekend I ran the Waitakeres for the first time!" That's the way it is with that run. The Commonwealth Games, fantastic, but the Waitakeres, a greater thing altogether.

This swimming program encapsulates the same character. Who swims 100x100m? Who swims ten weeks of 100kms? Who swims seven days, every week? Who swims sets of 2x3000m? Who swims three ten-kilometer sets every week? Only you! The physiological effect happens and stays with you for the rest of your life. You become stronger, fitter, faster and better than your under-trained competition – and so you should. The work you do is harder, longer, tougher and faster than anything they ever dreamed of. Sporting spin-doctors can rabbit on about training smarter, it's quality that counts, the benefits of sports science and all the other snake oil. Meantime you'll be halfway through another set of 100x100m and leaving them behind at about the same speed as they talk about it. The name of this chapter is an expression of Winston Churchill. Like a lot of his sayings it sounds pompous and slightly silly these days. But make no mistake – if you swim through all the preparation in this book, you will deserve success – guaranteed.

Jane Copland – swimmer, author and US College English major.

CHAPTER SIX
A LITERARY MEDLEY

Roger Robinson is three public things. He's a fine writer, a Professor of English and a winner of the Master's Section of the New York Marathon. He's actually probably much more than this, but for now these three will suffice. Half way through dinner at Arthur Lydiard's place recently, Roger began to develop the argument that sports writing and good writing seldom mixed. More needed to be done to provide sports books with literary merit. As Arthur opened the night's fifth bottle of red wine – he is a generous host – Roger was providing examples of sports books that passed the literary test and those that failed. One that failed was a book that he had looked forward to reading about some well-known runner. "Disappointingly," he said," The book turned out to be just a whole lot of training schedules and race commentaries." Even with all the wine I didn't have the courage to tell him my next sports book didn't even have the race commentaries, just training schedules.

However, what I did decide to do was hand over the last chapter of this book to Jane Copland, better known as New Zealand's best 200m breaststroke swimmer, and let her have a shot at mixing sport and writing. I hope you enjoy the result.

Butterfly

Where do butterflies go when it rains?
A little book I read once asked
Where do butterflies go?

And I can't remember if they told us where
And in the end, I don't really care.
Because I wear my butterfly into town
Strapped to my chest, and people stare.
It's made of sequins, and it's purple

And everything rhymes with that.

Midnight, Nice airport. For the benefit of Americans like Scott and Al, the aging televisions are tuned to Eurosport, broadcast in English.

'What are they doing?' asks Scott.
'I believe it's called rugby,' replies Al, chewing the edge of his polystyrene cup. 'Rugby, James?'

Rugby. The game of being trampled over by twenty-nine rampaging New Zealanders in front of 200 or so self-appointed experts in the pouring rain and cold grey mud until half-time when I was inevitably substituted for a larger, stupider form of humanity and sent to the bench to lick my wounds on my own. Yes, Al. Rugby.
'Who are they?' asks Scott.
'The ones in white are England and the others are Australia,' I say, wondering if maybe they are actually South Africa.
'Are there any rules?' asks Al.
'Not really.' I can't think of any in particular.
'Why do they stamp on their own players?' says Scott, watching closely. I'm thinking hard, but I can't quite remember.
'It's called a ruck...'

Al snorts into his coffee.
'It's all about getting down the field to score a try.'
'A what?' Scott laughs. 'A try?'
'Yeah, so you get to try and kick a goal.'
'So it's like a touch-down.'

I nod, agreeing. 'It is a touch-down.'
'And so then someone goes and kicks. Did you kick? Or did you ruck?'
'I ran around the outside looking for someone to pass me the ball.'
'And did they?'
'Not often. I was...that one. There. Number nine.'
'He's quite small,' says Scott.
'So am I,' I say.
'So you are,' says Al as he changes the channel.

Breaststroke

Three seconds later, my head came out of the water. There were lights in my eyes and a boiling rush. Eighteen seconds, although if things weren't going my way it would be longer. I thought, the quicker this is over, the better.

I was forced to think. Things behind me might catch me. I might be brought to face my past again. I was a bridesmaid a year ago in Dunedin. I was just a flower girl in Wellington, six months later. I was always turned away. Tonight, I thought, I was going to get married.

There was so much noise. Intermittent noise, when my head broke the surface. Human noise. Who was shouting? Shouting never saved anyone, never caught anyone, never won anything.

I was reminded of horses. I was reminded of many things. I was reminded of the horse race we watched that afternoon, from Hastings. They lined up and raced and the horses couldn't see anything but what was directly in front of them. Their jockeys whipped them until Cinder Bella went from last to first and passed the top three on the line to win, and Arthur was on his way to the double. I wonder if my father's friend Trevor is going to win the double tonight.

Sometimes I thought of music. I thought of the race from above, like a whirling camera at a pop show. I was underneath one of those whirling cameras two weeks ago in Sydney. My favorite Australian band was playing live at the Olympic Park. I shouted and waved at the whirling camera. It's not difficult to get on TV, just as it isn't difficult to sit and watch horse races on Saturday afternoons, or to shout and have me hear you, intermittently, not when I was underwater, searching down there for something, if only I had my eyes open. Maybe I did have my eyes open. I didn't see the lines or the ropes, but I saw all I should.

I saw the end. My past – the ugly, silver bridesmaids' dresses and those of the equally drab, brown flower girls – wanted me to stay. There were ten meters remaining and clear water either side of me. I swam, ecstatic with pain, into the wall.

Freestyle

A calendar, hanging on the wall of the kitchen, tells Yana there are fifteen days left in July, the seventh month of the year. Fifteen days, eight hours and ten minutes, although her father sets the clock on the microwave five minutes fast. 'Keeps you punctual,' Yana's mother echoes every now and then.

If there are fifteen days, eight hours and ten minutes left in July, and five months until January, then there are 168 days until the first day of Next Year.

Her father likes private schools. He, Ryan, likes clean red brick and green concrete, sharp pleats and crisp white collars. He belongs to the National Party and doesn't express an opinion on anything. He can talk for half an hour and say nothing at all.

Yana's father is passionate about rugby. He wants her to play netball. Whistle blowing Saturday mornings and red knees, mini-buses taking teams to Masterton, pilling bibs, stepping, goal defense; obstruction wing attack! At school, the A netball team sit at the front in Maths, the back in English, with their legs together in assembly but spread on Saturday night. They cut their fingernails for sport, but their claws are bared for special occasions.

From Yana's home in Wadestown, she can see Wellington Girls' College. Two main buildings, grey and orange, rise up from the safe and wise asphalt of Thorndon. Teal uniforms peel off trains at eight-fifteen. Chewing gum, shirts out, stretched jerseys and bags slung casually, casually, they are ogled by the Wellington College boys sweeping by on the bus. The third form College boys at the Highland Park shops give Yana the fingers, not realising how much she envies them.

Yana's bus winds through the suburbs, stopping intermittently to on-load more clean, green blazers and skirts. Wadestown has its dairy, its hairdresser and its church, but Wilton is less fortunate. The hill up to Karori is bordered by toi-toi; the fire station at the top almost ironic, mocking, as though someone is worried the native shrubbery might take light. The school gates, sturdy and far from chicken-wire, snarl 'No dogs allowed!' Was it too much to wish for that to be true?

The year's end is highly anticipated. On February the first she will not take the bus back to the school and its sabre-toothed population, the calendar in the kitchen replaced by a (surprise! Gosh, I'd never have guessed...) new edition offered on Christmas Day. An education, received for thousands of dollars, is being resented more and more with every blink of the clock, every turn of the bus wheel under Yana's well-covered, tartan bottom. She is to join the state school riffraff, her father grudgingly approving her escape to Thorndon's government funded paradise.

She knows the Karori fire station is there for a reason. One day she will watch them all burn.

Photo & Illustration Credits

Cover design: Jens Vogelsang
Inside and Back Cover Photos: Paul Errickson, Eric Hutchins,
p. 10: ASA Fotoagentur, p. 132, 176: Polar Electro GmbH
Coverphoto: ASA Fotoagentur

Wright/Gilmour

Swim to the Top

Arthur Lydiard takes to the Water

David Wright has been working with Arthur Lydiard on the translation of the latter's middle and distance running training schedules into a parallel system for swimmers. That process now reached the point where it may be established as the finest approach to correct swimming training that can be devised. The training programme is described in detailed guide-line swim schedules in this book.

136 pages
Two-color print
32 photos
Paperback, 5 3/4" x 8 1/4"
ISBN 1-84126-083-5
£ 9.95 UK/$ 14.95 US
$ 20.95 CDN/€ 14.90